Directory of Computer and High Technology Grants

Third Edition

A Reference Directory Identifying
Computer, Software, and High-Tech Grants
Available to Nonprofit Organizations

Research Grant Guides, Inc.
P.O. Box 1214
Loxahatchee, Florida 33470

Richard M. Eckstein
Publisher/Editor

Andrew J. Grant, Ph.D.
Writer/Grant Consultant

Research and Administrative Staff:

Nancy Moore
Lorraine Moynihan
Debra Reese
Amy L. Bachmann
Claire L. Eckstein

Marketing Representative:

Cathy J. Tosner
President
CJ Marketing

Printed in the U.S.A.

ISSN 1070-3950
ISBN 0-945078-13-7

Table of Contents

Preface

The third edition of the *Directory of Computer and High Technology Grants* will assist fund-raisers seeking grants for computers, software, and high technology.

The categories listed in the *Directory* include: computer grants, cultural programs, disabled, education (other than higher education), engineering, health organizations, higher education, high-tech office equipment (copy machine, fax machine, etc.), libraries, science, social services, software, and youth.

Funding sources may change their priorities and expenditure levels. Corporate foundations frequently respond to the general economy and may curtail their grantmaking programs until profits reach a satisfactory level. Don't be discouraged if your proposal is not funded on the first try.

To get started, use the *Directory* to research funding agencies that have previously awarded computer and technology grants to your type of organization. Be careful to remember that many foundations award grants only in their own geographic area. Geographic restrictions and grant range are listed when available to our research staff. Grant applicants should only review the foundation profiles listed within their own state. Next, send a brief letter to the funding agency to request a copy of their most recent grant guidelines, if they publish them. Guidelines issued by the funder should always be followed. Before writing a grant proposal, read the guidelines listed in "Proposal Writing Basics" beginning on page 20.

Several elements in a successful grant proposal include:

1) Uniqueness of proposal subject matter

2) A clear, well-written application

3) A realistic budget

4) Qualifications of the Project Director

5) Issues of concern to the proposed sponsor

If the proposal warrants, there should be a table of contents to guide the reviewer. A timetable depicting your projected progress may also be helpful. Try to present a readable, professional-looking proposal written in clear language that avoids jargon.

A Grant Seeker's Guide To The Internet: Revised And Revisited
by
Andrew J. Grant, Ph.D.
and Suzy D. Sonenberg, M.S.W.

The original version of "A Grant Seeker's Guide To The Internet" was published approximately two years ago in the Second Edition of the *Directory of Computer and High Technology Grants*. Much has changed since then. The Internet has become a household word and news of its expansion appears regularly in all sectors of the media. The World Wide Web, the hottest and fastest growing service on the Internet, didn't even exist when the original article appeared. The Web is a user-friendly method of accessing the most exciting features of the Internet.

Today Internet access is widely available at reasonable rates. Information about grants and other useful material for nonprofit organizations abounds. Any organization with a computer and modem will be able to conduct sophisticated searches and keep current right from their offices. In this update, we'll take a tour of what's new and expanded. We'll also point out some areas related to grants for which information is still scarce on the Internet.

Getting Connected

Perhaps the greatest change is today's easy accessibility to the Internet. The original article proposed several strategies for connecting. One suggestion was for nonprofits to approach a local university through which to obtain access. Today, there are many options at reasonable cost.

Dr. Grant is President of Grant Services Corp., a consulting firm specializing in grants development, proposal writing and computer networking. The firm is located in Woodbury, New York, and offers consulting services on a national basis. Dr. Grant has had a twenty-year academic career in grants development and research administration. He teaches proposal writing and grants management at Hofstra University.

Andrew Grant holds a Ph.D. in Public Administration from New York University. He also has an M.A. in Education and a Master of Urban Planning, both from NYU. His B.A. is from SUNY Binghamton. Dr. Grant's e-mail address is ajgrant@interramp.com.

Suzy Sonenberg has been Executive Director of the Long Island Community Foundation (an affiliate of The New York Community Trust) since March, 1988.

After receiving a Master's Degree in Social Work from Adelphi University in 1976, Ms. Sonenberg spent 8 years as a nonprofit administrator and grant seeker before joining the funding community. She has taught social policy on the graduate and undergraduate levels at Adelphi School of Social Work, and often appears as a guest lecturer on "fund-raising from foundations" at various institutions of higher learning in the New York Metropolitan area. Her e-mail address is suzylicf@aol.com.

There are several national and many local Internet service providers through which individuals and organizations can purchase an account. Service providers are companies specializing in making the Internet available through telephone dial-in systems. Costs are based on the number of hours of use. Most plans range from $20 to $30 per month for a base number of hours, usually twenty or thirty. For occasional use, there are plans for as little as $9 for nine hours per month. Usage above the base period is generally billed at $1.50 per hour in excess of that included in the plan. Recently, providers have begun to offer unlimited access for off-peak use, which usually means late nights and weekends. With careful monitoring of use, a nonprofit could limit its cost to the basic $20-$30 monthly fee. This is a reasonable investment considering the vast amount of information available. As we'll note in a later section, an Internet account could pay for itself many times if the organization finds it can cancel some of its subscriptions to printed resources now available on-line.

Finding an Internet provider also has become simple. There are advertisements in any computer magazine or daily newspaper and listings in the telephone directory. There are even several magazines devoted entirely to the Internet. Performance Systems International (PSI) in Herndon, Virginia and Netcom in San Jose, California are two of the largest providers. Their ads are easy to find. The national companies have many phone numbers all over the country; access is usually available with a local phone call. Obviously, a local provider also will minimize the cost of connecting. Not every locality will be able to avoid telephone toll charges, but before long this will change, too. Thus, cost is much less an obstacle.

In addition to service providers, the major on-line services now offer Internet access. On-line services are companies offering a variety of activities to customers who dial in. These can include, but are by no means limited to, computer hardware and software technical support, shopping, financial services, weather information, software sharing, hobbies and socializing. Familiar names are America Online, CompuServe and Prodigy. Each uses its own special access software.

These companies realized that they would become noncompetitive if they didn't expand to offer Internet access in addition to their other services. They are an excellent alternative to service providers, but tend to be a bit more costly. Typically, an on-line service currently charges $9.95 for five hours of access with a charge of $2.95 per hour beyond the first five. Connect charges add up quickly. For example, the same thirty hours available for $30 through PSI (not even including the unlimited off-peak usage) would cost $83.70 on the on-line services. The advantages are that they offer services other than just Internet accessibility, there are more local phone numbers and they tend to be easier to set up. Like the service providers, they advertise extensively and are easy to find.

The other issues to be considered are hardware and software. Nothing exotic is required. Even a 386 DOS machine with a relatively inexpensive modem can connect to the Internet. To take full advantage of the graphics, especially with the World Wide Web, a 486 or Macintosh with a speedy modem have become the standards of the day. The modem is a communications device that connects (either internally or externally) to the computer on one end and to the telephone line on the other. It transmits, through the phone lines, the data that appears on the screen as text and graphics. The fastest modems run at 28.8 kilobytes per second. The faster the modem, the less time it takes for the text and images to fill the screen. Excellent modems are available for as little as $200. The more expensive models have additional features, but if cost is a factor, a $200 28.8 modem will do just fine. An additional benefit is that most modems also double as computer fax machines and come with software that accesses all their features.

Whether one uses a service provider (like Netcom) or an on-line service (like America Online), special software is required. The on-line services provide the software for free, as do some service providers like Netcom. Other providers require the customer to purchase this software separately from a computer software vendor. The software includes several programs that serve as tools for working with the Internet. Internet Chameleon or Internet-In-A-Box cost between $79 and $100. They contain many of the most useful tools and are available from most retailers and mail-order vendors. Software, like the Netscape Web browser, which has been available free, can be downloaded (retrieved) from the Internet. It allows the user to access the World Wide Web and is considered a much better product than some of the browsers that come with retail software packages. All these programs are relatively easy to install and set up.

Internet Tools

Internet tools, or protocols as they are called, are a group of software programs that help search for, collect and display information. They are available either free or for purchase as noted in the preceding section. Increasing sophistication of the tools has made the Internet easier to use and more attractive to a wide range of people and organizations. Let's review the evolution of these tools to gain an understanding of what the Internet offers and what has changed.

When it first started, the Internet was a mechanism for scholars, mostly scientists, to share information and collaborate on studies. It didn't matter if the scholars were on the same campus or around the world. They were able to use the Internet to send each other messages and drafts of research papers at low cost and with great speed. The tools consisted of three basic protocols known as electronic mail (e-mail), telnet and ftp.

Electronic mail (e-mail) is one of the most popular Internet protocols. It allows Internet users to send messages to other users. E-mail is known as an asynchronous communications form. This means that the sender and recipient don't need to be connected at the same time for the message to be delivered. If the recipient is not logged on (connected) to the computer e-mail program, the message waits until the next time the user checks messages. By way of contrast, the telephone is a synchronous communications form—both parties need to be there in order for a conversation to take place. Adding an answering machine converts the phone to an asynchronous device.

E-mail is efficient and inexpensive. There is no cost in addition to that of the charges paid to the service provider or on-line service. Messages can be sent all over the world. They can be as short as one word or can contain the text of an entire article or paper. Delivery can be within minutes, but generally takes a few hours. Even when there is a great deal of traffic on the Internet, delivery is almost never longer than twenty-four hours.

Telnet is a protocol that allows users to sign onto other computers. There are many Internet sites that are public. That is, anyone can access the programs and information they contain. Generally, universities and some large libraries are public sites. If an individual, for example, needs to use a database, they would use telnet to "go to" the remote computer and use it as though they were at a terminal physically connected to that university or library.

Ftp stands for file transfer protocol. This tool allows anyone to connect to another computer and transfer files to or from it using their own PC. Many government agencies and some foundations, for example, are making their guidelines available on the Internet. With ftp, those guidelines can be printed and ready for use within minutes. Compare this with the weeks it can take to request and receive them in the mail.

Originally, Internet protocols required knowledge of commands that had to be typed into the computer. Information was displayed on the screen only as text. When using telnet and ftp, it was necessary first to locate the information being sought through additional search protocols or through word-of-mouth.

For example, about two years ago one of the authors needed a copy of the United States Constitution for a graduate course about the grants system. He could have used a duplicating machine to make copies from an almanac, but that would have been inefficient and the copies would not have been very good. He also could have had it retyped, but that would have been even more inefficient. He thought that someone, probably another university faculty member, must have a copy of the Constitution somewhere on the Internet. Using a search protocol named Archie (from the comics, like Veronica, another Internet search tool), he entered the keywords US Constitution. After some time a long list of "hits" appeared in the form of ftp locations. Many were articles about the Constitution, but a few were copies of the document itself. Using the ftp protocol, he transferred to the first site on the list indicating a copy of the Constitution and retrieved the item—it was in Russian. Several other sites did not offer public access. Finally he found a public site with a copy of the Constitution in English and retrieved it. It was then sent via e-mail to the students. The total time was under an hour, far less than that required to duplicate twenty-five copies for the class. Plus, there was now a copy on the hard drive (with a back-up copy on disc, of course) to use for future classes.

Until a short while ago, very few people outside of universities and the scientific community had the access or the ability to get much use from the Internet (this was still primarily the case as recently as the publication of the first edition of this article). The tools noted above—e-mail, telnet and ftp—are still the basis of all operations on the Internet, but new, additional software protocols that incorporate them have made it much easier to navigate on-line. This greater ease of use has been responsible for the extraordinary expansion of the Internet.

The Internet for Everyone

The first great improvement was *gopher* software. Gopher eliminates the need to know and use ftp and telnet commands. It uses menus to move around the Internet. A menu is displayed as a text list of numbered items on the screen. Gopher started on university based systems, but it is also found among the tools sold in Internet software suites. After typing the word "gopher" at the command prompt, the user would be greeted by a list of topics, usually about the host university. There may be information about faculty, registration, campus events, financial aid, and happenings in the surrounding community. This is far from an exhaustive list. The particular items will vary from site to site. One element found in almost all gopher lists is an item called *Other Gopher Servers Around the World*. Selecting it (by typing its number at the cursor or highlighting it and pressing the *Enter* key) would bring up another menu listing major world regions. Selecting any of these brings up yet another menu of regions within that area. For example, one could do this until it resulted in a list of all the U.S. states and territories, plus one or two general categories. Selecting a state would bring up another menu of all the sites in the state with gopher programs running on their computers, known as servers. Selecting a particular site again brings up the menu for that site. Eventually, the menu items would be differentiated as additional menus or documents. These documents can be downloaded into the user's computer. They usually are text documents, but could also include computer programs or graphics files containing pictures or other images.

The word gopher elicits two images. One is the linguistic construction "go fer" referring to the software's ability to retrieve items on the Internet. The other is to the garden animal, which burrows deeper and deeper into the ground, similar to the software's use of menus through which the user must burrow to get to the information desired. Gopher software is nothing more than a way of using telnet and ftp without the need to issue commands. Each time an item is selected and the screen brings it up, the user is being transferred (i.e. using telnet) to a remote computer or directory. Each time a document is selected for downloading, the user is activating the ftp protocol. Gopher, with its use of the point and click menu system instead of issued commands, made the Internet much more accessible to many more people.

It also introduced the concept of browsing the Internet. Rather than zeroing in on a particular piece of information, as the author did in his search for the Constitution, users could now simply move from menu to menu, site to site, university or organization to university or organization and browse around just to see what may be interesting and available.

Gopher, however, was only the beginning. The single most significant event in propelling the Internet into widespread use was the development of the World Wide Web (WWW). The Web was born with the invention of a product called *Mosaic*. Mosaic is known as a Web browser, and takes ease of use far beyond that made possible by gopher. It made advances in several areas. First, it pioneered the use of hypertext. In a hypertext document displayed on the computer screen, most text is displayed in one color, and every now and then a group of words may be displayed in another color. For example, if the document is predominantly in black text, the hypertext may show up as blue. Each instance of hypertext is a link to another computer site or different area within the same host. Using the mouse (Mosaic and other Web browsers are used only with graphical interfaces like Windows or the Macintosh—for DOS environments, a text based browser called LYNX is available) to click on the hypertext transfers the user to that site. Thus, the ability to telnet to a remote computer had been reduced to a single mouse click. Similarly, where the hypertext link refers to a document, program or image, that item can be downloaded with a single mouse click.

Another advance was the ability of Mosaic to display graphic images with photographic quality, and to a lesser extent to play sound files. The Internet, almost overnight, became significantly easier to use and vastly more interesting. After approximately two years, several companies have released other Web browsers with capabilities far beyond the original Mosaic. The most popular is *Netscape*, which can be obtained on the Internet for free or purchased in retail stores for approximately $40. The current version includes a full e-mail program, audio player and newsgroup reader.

The Web's easy navigation and downloading features created increasing demand to get onto the Internet. As more users signed up with an increasing number of providers and on-line services, more and more governmental, commercial, nonprofit and educational organizations began offering services on the Web. Web sites are known as home pages. They include text and graphics and are developed with the use of *hypertext markup language* (HTML). The address of the site is known as its Universal Resource Locator (URL). Thus, one can browse through the Web by clicking on links to move from home page to home page or one can enter the URL in the browser software to go directly to the site. Once at the site, there inevitably are links to other related sites, making it easy to locate resources of interest. Netscape also has a search feature that uses keywords to describe the search topic. The search results are displayed as hypertext links. A user can conduct a search, and then simply click on the listed sites to get there in a matter of seconds.

Many publications, including books, directories, and magazine and newspaper articles routinely list interesting sites. Professional organizations are establishing home pages to help members identify resources. URLs are written in a specific format, which at first may feel a bit awkward, but becomes second nature in no time. For example, to get to the Netscape* home page to download the software, the user would enter the URL, http:// home.netscape.com/ in the browser software (if there is no other Web browser available, the software can be downloaded by going to Netscape's ftp site). The http:// is a standard preface used in all URLs. Some home pages are interactive. Federal Express allows customers to check on the status of a package right on the Internet. Go to http:// www.fedex.com/cgi-bin/track_it and there will be a space to enter the package tracking number. In seconds, the screen displays where the package is and gives the name of the person signing for it if it has already been delivered.

Grant Seeking on the Internet

Grant seekers in nonprofit organizations of all sizes and interests can use the Internet to learn about available grant opportunities. The Web certainly is a robust resource, and we shall concentrate on pointing out some helpful sites in the balance of the article. But grant seekers should not overlook other important features available on the Internet. E-mail listserve lists and newsgroups are vital sources for networking. Listserves are discussion groups of people with similar interests—corporate and foundation relations for example. By sending a subscription request to a listserve, a user will be able to write to all members of that list with a single e-mail posting. Each subscriber receives in e-mail all the messages sent to the list. Newsgroups are similar, but instead of receiving the list postings in e-mail, the user needs to access the newsgroup through software for that purpose and browse through the messages. As noted above, Netscape includes a newsgroup reader.

*See page 14 for a complete list of all referenced Internet home pages.

The first question, of course, is Where does one find out how to locate mailing lists (these use e-mail to link large numbers of people who are interested in a topic), newsgroups and URLs? There are several comprehensive lists of resources on the Internet. An excellent place to start is a home page called "Internet Resources for Nonprofits" (http://www.ai.mit.edu/people/ellens/Non/online.html)—case sensitive. This excellent page lists hundreds of other home pages, newsgroups and listserves directly or indirectly related to grant seeking. Another is "URLs for Grant Seekers" (http://faraday.clas.virginia.edu/~ebf9q/url_list.html). University development and grants offices often provide valuable information with links to foundation, corporate and other information links. A great example is found at Amherst College's development office (http://www.amherst.edu/~develop/resources/resonlin/intsource.html). Another good source is The Foundation Center home page (http://fdncenter.org/).

By consulting just these four home pages, a grant seeker will find references to many more sites. Many of the sites appear in various places. Seeing the sites repeating as one moves among the home pages is a good indication that the search has been comprehensive. That is, the grant seeker will have located most of the useful sites. The beauty of the Web is that a handful of sites often lead to as much information as is available.

By far the greatest volume of information on the Web about grant opportunities will be found on government home pages. Recently, the US Government Printing Office made several of its publications available on-line for free. Full text searches and downloading articles from the *Federal Register* and *Congressional Record* can be accessed from http://www.access.gpo.gov/su_docs/. Considering the subscription rate for the paper *Federal Register* is $575, this service alone could pay for a year's worth of Internet access.

The Federal Government's bible of funding opportunities, *The Catalog of Federal Domestic Assistance* (CFDA), is at gopher://portfolio.stanford.edu:1970/1100334 (even though this is a gopher address, it can be accessed with a Web browser—there's no longer a need to run a separate *gopher* program). Many federal agencies have their own home pages with information about their programs. A few that readers of this Directory will find useful are: National Science Foundation (http://www.nsf.gov/), the National Institutes of Health (http://www.nih.gov/), the U.S. Education Department (http://www.ed.gov/), the National Endowment for the Humanities (http://www.neh.fed.us/) and the U.S. Information Agency (http://www.usia.gov/).

The URLs in this section will enable a grant seeker to find much of the information available as well as information related to specific interests, such as health, education, the arts, social services and almost any other topic of interest. All these sites are free. There are others through which their owners offer grants search services for a subscription fee. One especially interesting site to institutions of higher education is "Academe Today" (http://chronicle.com/), published by *The Chronicle of Higher Education*. It is available only with a user name and password, but these are provided to all subscribers of *The Chronicle*. "Academe Today" offers access to this publication's large, searchable database of grants that have been awarded to colleges and universities for the past five years. It also has a searchable database of all articles published in *The Chronicle* for a five-year period. That and the weekly job postings are well worth the price of a subscription.

Despite this enormous amount of information, there are still notable absences on the Internet, particularly the foundation world. Foundations have not established a presence, as we explain in the following section.

Where are the Foundations?

Despite the fact that they have the resources to make a significant impact on the Internet, private grantmakers have been reluctant to get on-line. The results of an informal poll conducted in the summer of 1995 by a publication of the national Council on Foundations appear to support our observations that members of the foundation community have been slower to embrace the opportunities offered by the new technology than have been those who seek their support.

As this is written, fewer than three dozen foundations nationwide have sites on the World Wide Web, although this number is growing from month to month. Those foundations that are there in the forefront tend to be the larger and nationally focused foundations such as MacArthur (gopher://gopher.macfdn.org:3016/11/), Carnegie (http://www.carnegie.org/carnegie/), Rockefeller (http://www.rbf.org/rbf/), and the Robert Wood Johnson Foundation (gopher://nicol.jvnc.net:70/11/Hosted/RWJF), or those with a particular understanding of or interest in communications technology such as the Benton Foundation (http://www.cdinet.com/Benton/homepage.html) and several corporate foundations.

Their Web sites tend to be purely informational and non-interactive. That is, one can gather information that the foundation has placed there about its mission, program, structure, and grantmaking. In some cases there is a response box for limited feedback, but in most instances there is not even an e-mail address to which one might direct further inquiries. In addition we did not find, on a cursory review of the existing foundation Web sites, any foundations that indicate a willingness to receive proposals via e-mail.

Conversations with representatives of a number of these foundations reveal that the sites were either established with outside help or through the expertise of a single staff member who is solely responsible for on-line communication with grant seekers because only he or she has the expertise among foundation staff. On further examination it seems likely that this lack of staff knowledge or comfort with existing and emerging communications technologies has been one of the more serious current inhibitors to the broader use of this technology by the entire foundation community.

At the 1995 annual conference of the Council on Foundations, a cyber (slang for the Internet) track was incorporated into the 3-day program. Well attended, but not stunningly so, this track featured an array of presentations designed to entice, educate and excite funders about the technological revolution, and to encourage their participation both through their grantmaking and their own on-line activities. While many responded positively to the presentations, the question most often repeated at the end was, Why should we get on-line? To what end? Unfortunately, the best answer offered was, "To provide broader access to your foundation." Unfortunate because many foundations, doing a lot more work with far fewer staff than one might imagine, are seriously concerned that the type of broad access implied by a Web site might be their undoing in terms of volume of inquiries and requests for funding.

Nevertheless, as slow as the foundation community is to move in new directions, this particular tide is gaining momentum and new sites are to be found on the Web on a regular basis. What does this mean to grant seekers? Well, for one thing it means being able to research foundations from their offices as opposed to going to a library.

It also, through the use of hypertext links, broadens the context for the grant seeker. For example, a quick check of The Foundation Center's grantmaker information page (http://fdncenter.org/grantmaker/contents.html) offers the reader not only information about The Foundation Center's services and a glossary of grantmakers, but hypertext connections (one-click transfers) to information about how to research foundations, a short course in proposal writing, an explanation and copy of a widely accepted common application form, giving trends, and alternative funding resources.

Another thing to think about is that there is now a unique opportunity to interact with funders in a venue that hasn't yet been layered with protective screens. The survey described earlier in this article yields the interesting information that an equal proportion of grantmakers and grant seekers are currently using e-mail—52% of those surveyed. Consequently, whether or not foundations have set up Web pages, many are already on-line and directly accessible in a way that they are not via telephone or through other connections.

The question of whether funders themselves are on-line is sometimes less interesting than the question of how they feel about supporting grant seekers in their efforts to get on-line. Common wisdom however, supports the theory that the more sophisticated the funder in the use of technology, the more likely that funder is to make grants for these purposes.

There is much concern and discussion in the foundation community, particularly among those foundations that understand the implications of communications technology, about providing access to people who are out of the loop so that the "information super highway" doesn't become the civil rights issue of the 21st Century. The focus is on making certain that not only the technological elite (i.e. people and organizations with computers) have access, particularly as more public service activities (like the *Federal Register*) become available on-line and as dialogue begins to take place in cyberspace.

Grant seekers hoping to find technology grants would do well to approach those foundations that have demonstrated an understanding of its possibilities through their own behaviors. One potential source is the "Apple Partners in Education Program" (http://www.info.apple.com/education/). In the case of those grantmakers that are still technologically uninformed, an educational process will be necessary and may be daunting. On the other hand, those foundations on the cutting edge of this issue like the Benton Foundation, are good resources. That foundation has, on its Web page, an evolving list of interesting examples of how nonprofits have used communications technology.

It is clear that use of the Internet will continue to grow, especially as its commercial value is fully understood by more companies and industries. Information available to grant seekers is already extensive, despite the reluctance on the part of the foundation community. Our references to home pages will get the grant seeker started on a journey incredible for its efficiency and sheer volume of information. Enjoy the trip!

Internet Web sites (or home pages) identified in this article include:

1. Netscape
   http://home.netscape.com/

2. Federal Express
   http://www.fedex.com/cgi-bin/track_it

3. Internet Resources for Nonprofits
   http://www.ai.mit.edu/people/ellens/Non/online.html

4. URLs for Grant Seekers
   http://faraday.clas.virginia.edu/~ebf9q/url_list.html

5. Amherst College's Development Office
   http://www.amherst.edu/~develop/resources/resonlin/intsource.html

6. The Foundation Center
   http://fdncenter.org/

7. The *Federal Register* and the *Congressional Record*
   http://www.access.gpo.gov/su_docs/

8. The *Catalog of Federal Domestic Assistance*
   gopher://portfolio.stanford.edu:1970/1100334

9. National Science Foundation
   http://www.nsf.gov/

10. National Institutes of Health
    http://www.nih.gov/

11. US Education Department
    http://www.ed.gov/

12. National Endowment for the Humanities
    http://www.neh.fed.us/

13. US Information Agency
    http://www.usia.gov/

14. Academe Today published by *The Chronicle of Higher Education*
    http://chronicle.com/

15. John D. and Catherine T. MacArthur Foundation
    gopher://gopher.macfdn.org:3016/11/

16. Carnegie Corporation of New York
    http://www.carnegie.org/carnegie/

17. Rockefeller Brothers Fund
    http://www.rbf.org/rbf/

18. Robert Wood Johnson Foundation
    gopher://nicol.jvnc.net:70/11/Hosted/RWJF

19. Benton Foundation
    http://www.cdinet.com/Benton/homepage.html

20. The Foundation Center
    http://fdncenter.org/grantmaker/contents.html

21. Apple Partners in Education Program
    http://www.info.apple.com/education/

Computers and the Nonprofit Organization
by
Jon Rosen

The computer is probably the most useful, but underutilized device in offices today. In this article we will look at the hardware and the software you need to automate your office effectively.

Nearly any computer that you buy today is powerful enough to do the fundamentals. After all, it doesn't take much processing power to replace your typewriter; not even the fastest typist can outpace current word processors. Today, however, computers are much more than word processors. You can use them to create and to view multimedia extravaganzas. Rather than trips to the library, grant information is available at your computer on CD-ROMs or on the Internet (see "A Grant Seeker's Guide to the Internet" beginning on page 5). Computers enable you to track your donors with database software and larger offices can use computer e-mail to replace interoffice memos. There are thousands of software programs available yet most people will never venture out to discover more for fear of "ruining something." Instead, they get by with the minimum needed to do their jobs because they have not mastered their computer.

Which Computer to Buy?

When choosing a computer, don't rely on a computer store to recommend a purchase. Why? The salespeople at most computer stores probably are not knowledgeable enough about both Macs (Macintoshes) and PCs (IBM compatibles) to make informed recommendations. Instead, review computer magazines and speak with colleagues about their experiences. Whether you are choosing a Macintosh or an IBM compatible, look at advertisements and select a model that is at least the middle of the road in terms of speed. Choosing a slower, less expensive computer could mean that your purchase will soon be obsolete.

There are a number of issues that control the overall power of a computer, or the speed at which it can perform tasks. The three most important ones are: the type of microprocessor, the rated speed of the processor and the amount of RAM.

At the heart of every desktop and portable computer is a microprocessor. If you can visualize your computer as a data factory, the microprocessor (sometimes called a CPU, or Central Processing Unit) would be the foreman. Data enters and leaves. It is manipulated and transformed. The CPU directs all of this activity. Particularly during the past 10 years, the CPU has evolved and become more powerful. Intel and Motorola, the two pri-

Jon Rosen is President of Intellitec, a computer consulting firm that specializes in customized multi-user database solutions and other computer-related services. Previously, he managed the Information Systems Department of a Fortune 500 corporation subsidiary. Mr. Rosen has more than fifteen years experience in the computer industry. His e-mail address is jonro@aol.com.

mary manufacturers of these computer chips, designated each successive member of their CPU families with increasing numbers. For Intel, the chip sequence was designated 8086, 80286, 80386, 80486 and the Pentium (80586). In the Motorola family, it was the 68000, 68020, 68030, 68040 and now the PowerPC 601 and 604. Is there much performance difference between the two rival chip corporations? At the moment, Motorola's PowerPC appears to have a bit of an edge, but both corporations are fairly well-matched and tend to pass each other back and forth. Motorola claims that in another year or so, their PowerPC will leapfrog the Intel line. Intel claims that is unlikely. In the future, both are expected to remain competitive with each other.

The speed at which these CPUs process data is measured by the speed of their clocks in millions of cycles per second, or MHz (megahertz). The speed of the chips that control the clock has been steadily increasing over the years. The first commercial microprocessors ran at 1 MHz. Current models run at over 120 MHz. As software becomes more sophisticated, greater demands are placed on the CPU. For this reason, you will not want to skimp on processing power when making your computer purchase.

The last item, RAM (Random Access Memory), is simple to understand. It is the electronic storage that holds your programs and data *while you are running them.* 16 MB (megabytes, or million bytes) or more is recommended for today's computers. Utility programs like RAM Doubler can make your computer think it has more RAM than it really does and usually does not adversely affect performance. Hard disks are more permanent storage for your computer. Unlike RAM, they store programs and data when your computer is off. Because the capacity of hard disks has increased dramatically in recent years, most computers will have sufficient storage for your needs.

Incidentally, if you spend much of your time on the road, you should consider a portable computer. Most of these machines, while not as expandable, have the power of their desktop siblings. In addition, you can often add a regular monitor, so you do not have to spend your days staring at a 10" LCD (Liquid Crystal Display), although active matrix LCD displays often rival the quality of CRTs (Cathode Ray Tube, or standard TV picture tube).

MACs or IBM Compatibles?

Should you purchase a Mac or an IBM compatible PC? While Microsoft's Windows 95 has made strides in closing the gap between the IBM compatible PC and the Mac/OS, it is this writer's opinion that the Mac still wins the ease-of-use award. Mac users can install new hardware like printers and hard disks more easily. Mac software is generally easier to use because the operating system is more intuitive than that of the PC. Mac users require less training than their PC colleagues. However, nearly 90% of all computers sold are IBM compatibles and most of the grant software is IBM compatible. Fortunately, software is available to convert Mac documents to PC and PC to Mac. More cross-platform options are noted in a later discussion on peripheral equipment.

Software Options

What type of software will you run? The most common types of software are word processing, spreadsheets, databases, presentation software and accounting software. Other applications you may run are e-mail, networking (connecting computers together) and World Wide Web (Internet browsers).

One word here about presentation software. Today, more than ever, there is great competition among nonprofits for financial resources. Presentation software allows you to use graphics to dramatize your position which can add a very persuasive element to your request for funds.

When purchasing the standard programs you use day in and day out, you have a choice between *software suites* and *integrated software*. The most popular software suite is Microsoft Office. This includes Word (word processing), Excel (spreadsheet), PowerPoint (presentation software), and for DOS/Windows computers, Access (database software). While very popular, such office suites are often overkill. They have so many features that they require bloated amounts of memory. On the other hand, integrated software packages like ClarisWorks or MicrosoftWorks join together word processing, spreadsheet, database, draw/paint software and communications software into a single well-integrated package. These are less expensive, use far less memory and usually have all the features you need. The point is that Excel and Lotus are extremely powerful spreadsheets with features that an MBA might never use. If you require such detailed financial planning, then by all means purchase the tool that does the job properly for you. If, however, you are like most users, you should consider the easier-to-use integrated packages. Incidentally, all of these software packages are available for both the Mac and the PC.

Good grant-related software has been available for years. Perhaps the most important piece of grant software your nonprofit will use is a database. A database should model the work flow of an organization and track all of the essential information as it is being processed. As a nonprofit, you will use a database to track donors, report on the amount each has donated, record the length of time since the last gift, compute whether the contributions are increasing or decreasing, generate letters, etc. How does the database do all of these things and more? A database is actually a computer program that is dedicated to storing, modifying, retrieving and printing data.

You may decide to purchase a grant software program that has already been written. While most of the bugs or programming defects, have already been corrected, you lose some flexibility. Typically, you will be forced to change some things about the way you conduct your business when you buy *off-the-shelf*. Nevertheless, there are many good grant-related programs available.

Rather than purchase existing software, you may decide to contract with a computer consultant to write what is called a custom program. This person, for a fee, learns how your organization conducts its business and writes a program using a database language that meets those needs. There are dozens, if not hundreds, of database languages, but some of the more common ones are: FileMaker, FoxPro, Access, Approach, Oracle and Informix. Most consultants have one or two favorites that they work with.

The Role of the Computer Consultant

Once you purchase your computer(s), who is going to set them up, install software and network them? If you have more than one computer, you will want to connect them so that everyone can share information. This is called networking. While it does not have to be complicated, usually a computer professional is needed to network multiple computers. Most computer stores do not offer these services. When they do, they often provide only a small amount of what you need, or they may be rather expensive. If you are large enough or fortunate enough to have an employee who can do this work for you, then consider yourself lucky. Computers are not incomprehensible, but it takes time to read software manuals and figure out how to set things up. Your time may be better spent running your nonprofit.

Computer consultants are organizations or individuals who can meet these needs. Like most consultants, however, there is a wide range of skill level, experience and price from which to chose. The first thing to do when looking for this service is to ask for referrals and recommendations from colleagues who use computer consultants. If they are satisfied with the level of service from their consultant, then you probably will be as well. If you purchased your computer from a store, the salespeople may have a recommendation. You might also call the manufacturer of your equipment or the publisher of your software to see if they have certified consultants in your area. Once you purchase computer equipment, you will rapidly become dependent upon it. Therefore, you should make certain that you can establish a good rapport with the individual you select and that they can keep things running smoothly.

Some Notes on Peripheral Equipment

There is something else that you should purchase with your computer(s)—surge protectors and battery backups. One of the leading causes of computer problems is the countless unseen power surges and brownouts that often corrupt a power supply. A battery backup should at least be used on the server (the computer that holds your database and other information treasures). When there is a power outage, the battery backup will keep your computer running for several minutes, long enough for you to do an orderly shutdown. Without battery backup, if you lose power while you are saving a file, the results can be disastrous.

That brings me to data backups. Sooner or later, something catastrophic *will* happen to your valuable data. Perhaps you will delete an important file by mistake. Maybe your disk drive will fail. Perhaps a leak from the floor above will find its way into your computer's case, causing unusual sound effects before your computer's demise. If you do daily backups you can rest easy. You need to select a backup medium that is reasonably quick and easy. I recommend tape backups for several reasons. The cost of the tape is low, so you can have a separate backup for each day of the week. Tapes are small and portable. One of the most common types of tape is called DAT. They store a lot of data at a reasonable price. It's also a very good idea to keep at least one of the backups away from your premises. You could have a hundred backups next to the computer, but in case of fire, they will be destroyed with everything else. The only other practical method of backing up your data is to use removable cartridges. The advantage to cartridges is that you can use them as additional hard disk storage. The disadvantage is that cartridges are usually more expensive to purchase.

Because you are going to sit and stare at a computer screen for long periods of time, selecting a good monitor is important. If you can, preview a few different designs and select one that is easy on your eyes. Due to economies of scale, nearly all monitors are color. You can purchase portrait monitors, which approximate the dimensions of a piece of paper, but the most common (and least expensive) monitors are the standard rectangular ones. The most common size is 13"-14" inches measured diagonally. However, bigger is better if you will be using several programs at a time. The price of 17" monitors has dropped dramatically and they should definitely be considered.

Another computer peripheral you will need is a CD-ROM (Compact Disc Read-Only Memory). It is a high capacity storage disc. CD-ROMs look like regular music CDs, but contain computer programs and data. Today, nearly all computers are available with a built-in CD-ROM drive. It is recommended that you own one. Many programs and software updates are distributed by CD-ROM. They are inexpensive and reliable.

If you want to communicate with other computers in a remote location or use the Internet or another on-line service, you will need a modem. A modem is an electronic device that converts computer data into tones that can be sent over telephone lines. A modem and computer on the other end of the phone line convert those tones back into data. While many computers come with a modem, if you purchase one separately, get the fastest one you can. The faster you can move information, the better.

If you have a computer, you will most certainly need a printer. There are many options available for printers in a wide price range. Most people purchase either an inkjet printer or a laser printer. An inkjet printer sprays microscopic droplets of ink at the paper. A laser printer creates a high-resolution document. Both offer excellent quality. For large print volumes of more than 2,000 pages per month, you should definitely own a laser printer. For inexpensive color document production, you should purchase an inkjet printer.

Incidentally, earlier we discussed a computer purchase as though it would be either a Mac or a PC. But what if you currently have *both* Macs and PCs in your office? If so, don't worry. Today with a little forethought, they can be networked to share data without much trouble. The ability to read DOS disks is part of the Mac's system software, and there are several programs available that convert documents to Mac or PC. Programs like SoftPC allow you to run all PC Windows programs on your Macintosh and many programs, like Microsoft Word, allow you to read and write documents created under either the Mac or PC versions of their software.

Carrying networks a step further, there are now programs available that can be shared simultaneously by different computer brands. An example is a database program that allows both the Mac operator and the Windows operator to work in the same file at the same time. The cross-platform environment is available for printers, as well. DOS, Windows, and Mac users can share some printers, though not all.

Automating your nonprofit can provide better control over the organization and more efficient deployment of your resources. Successfully computerizing your organization, however, requires some time and thought. If you carefully consider your needs, purchase the proper hardware and software and make sure it is set up properly, you will find the experience a rewarding one.

Proposal Writing Basics
by
Andrew J. Grant, Ph.D.

Despite the availability of excellent references on the subject, proposal writing still seems an elusive art. Many of my colleagues working in foundations, corporations and government agencies despair at the poor quality of proposals they receive.

Proposals that fail to communicate effectively jeopardize the support that might be granted to an otherwise excellent project. Competition for funds is fierce. Many worthwhile projects must be declined because so many organizations pursue the limited dollars available. Poorly written proposals simply make it easy for the funder to reject the request; there are too many good ones to consider. For the pressured funder, it is impractical to spend time trying to make sense of unclear proposals.

I will add my voice to those who have written about this subject. Perhaps the best place to begin is with some fundamental, axiomatic observations about the process.

Some Truths That Should Be Self-Evident

• Research, not writing, is the first step. Funders have specific interests. These must be researched. Proposals should be submitted only to those sources that have articulated a priority in the type of project to be undertaken by the applicant. To do otherwise is like going shopping for groceries in a hardware store. The response can only be, "You're in the wrong place."

• Proposal writing requires a good writer. Communicating in clear, precise English assumes talent that not everyone possesses. Sometimes a proposal writer is in the wrong job. I've seen this more than occasionally in the training seminars I conduct. Although proposal writing is an excellent way to enter the fund-raising profession, it's not for everyone. Skills must be assessed accurately by the employer and job seeker. Writing is only one specialty required in fund-raising. People uncomfortable with writing can find many other rewarding career paths in professional fund-raising.

• Follow directions. Many funders provide specific instructions on what they want in a submission. If such directions exist, they should be adhered to without deviation. Frequently, however, there are no specific guidelines. For such cases the following outline provides a model of what should be contained in a proposal. The model is basic and flexible enough to accommodate different writing styles.

Starting: The Most Difficult Part

Questions that are asked frequently are, How should the proposal begin? and What is the best way to introduce the subject? The opening paragraph is of vital importance. It must set the stage and interest the reader enough to make him or her want to know more. All this in two or three sentences.

A most effective way to do this is to begin with a general or global statement of the problem to be addressed. Let's use the example of a project to provide neighborhood transportation for people with disabilities.

For example:
"The absence of accessible transportation constitutes a serious obstacle to people with disabilities in performing the routine tasks of everyday life."

This opening sentence would be followed by two or three other short statements. Their purpose is to focus the general issue to be addressed in the context of the local environment. These statements serve the purpose of describing how this issue manifests itself in the particular situation that is the subject of the proposal. The entire introduction should occupy no more than a half page of a three-page letter or a full page of a five-page formal proposal. Included might be some statistics descriptive of the severity of the problem and the population to be served.

Who Are You? Dealing From Strength

The second paragraph or section should describe the agency or organization proposing to conduct the project. The most important thing to remember here is not to assume any knowledge on the part of the reader. It is easy to become too familiar with an issue or organization. The effect on the proposal when this happens is an inadequate description. That's fatal to the case. The prospective funder must have a clear idea of precisely who the applicant is.

A good way to handle this section is to write several descriptions of the organization in advance. They should be of varying length. Taking time to do this results in a final description that presents the agency in its most favorable light.

That brings up another vital consideration. The proposing agency must convince the funder that it is the best choice to conduct a project dealing with the subject issue. Using our example of a transportation program, the description should touch upon the following items:

- Knowledge of the client population
- Knowledge of the geographic area to be served
- Experience in providing the service proposed
- Familiarity with the issue
- Qualifications of the staff
- Acceptance in the community

If an agency cannot present a compelling capability statement without exaggerating, it needs to revaluate its reasons for seeking funds for the project. Funders strive to invest in organizations that have the ability to put grants to maximum use. This description of capabilities, therefore, is probably the most important information to be covered in a proposal.

How Much Will It Cost?

This is no place to be bashful. The amount of money requested should be indicated as early as possible in the proposal. Ideally it should be included in the first paragraph. The dollar request says a lot about the project. It establishes limits. It tells the funder the extent of its participation. It says something about cost effectiveness. Finally, if the request is realistic, not too high or low for the funder to whom it's directed, it tells the funder that the applicant has done his or her homework.

What Will Be Different?

Until now we've been carefully setting the stage. We've prepared the reader to be interested in the project, which now must be described. What are the goals? How will it work? Who will benefit? Who will do the work? What will be accomplished?

In order for the description to be compelling, the project must have been well thought out. The heart of a good proposal is a good project. When the program has been well planned, this part of the proposal is easy to write. If that's not the case, the project planning must be reexamined. Often, project weaknesses become exposed in the act of attempting a written description that simply won't flow.

Other Considerations

Because writing styles are so individual, proposals will vary even if they are based on a common model. In all cases, the project itself will determine what is appropriate to include and omit. For example, a statement regarding how the agency will measure success is important. The formality and complexity of the evaluation design, however, will vary greatly.

Many funders like to know whose company they are keeping. It's often useful to indicate what other sources of funding there are.

Finally, each organization has ancillary materials that can be appended to a proposal. A certificate of nonprofit status and an audited financial statement are standards. Other attachments should be included only if they make a contribution to the case.

In closing, it bears noting that proposal writing takes practice. It is a skill that requires development. This model provides a guide to the structure of a proposal. Substance and style are very much a function of the individual writer.

Take Nothing for Granted
by
Chris Petersen

Last year, according to the AAFRC Trust for Philanthropy, foundations and corporations contributed some $16 billion to America's nonprofit organizations.

While this doesn't compare to the amount given by individuals—a whopping $114 billion—it nevertheless confirms the wisdom of having a balanced development program that includes grant seeking. For the untutored, there are a host of seminars and books on the subject. But in reality, there's no special mystique about proposal writing. If you have a worthy idea, a solid organization behind you, the time to conduct research, and the ability to communicate in writing, you can prepare a successful proposal. However, the time-consuming task of writing proposals can be made easier, and more profitable, if you adopt the principles and techniques outlined below.

Understand that writing your proposal is only one aspect of the process.

It goes without saying that, to win a grant, you need a persuasively written proposal. But that doesn't mean you should spend all or even most of your time on the actual writing. Grant seeking is a *process*, often an extended one, that also involves planning, research, personal contact, and follow up. What you do before and after writing and submitting your proposal is often more germane than the "i's" you dot or the "t's" you cross.

Consider but one hypothetical. If you had the choice of a personal contact with a high-ranking funding officer *or* a flawlessly written proposal, which would you select? Experienced grant seekers would almost always opt for the former. Grant seeking isn't grant writing alone; it is a thorough and thoughtful process and must be viewed in this context.

Present your organization credibly.

While some funders will give to an organization they don't know—because the project has special appeal—they nevertheless want to be assured their money is going to a credible organization with strong leadership. Early in the grant seeking process, therefore, you must view your organization from the perspective of a funder who knows little or nothing about you.

How can you demonstrate to this funder that your cause has merit? It will demand a great deal of thought and articulation on your part. You will need to speak confidently about the mission of your organization, the people you serve, the ways you are different from other organizations, the quality of your management, your fiscal record, and the results you have achieved.

This article is reprinted with permission from Contributions, P.O. Box 336, Medfield, MA 02052-0336. Their telephone number is (508) 359-0019.

This information must be at your fingertips so that as you learn about particular funders, you will know which aspects of your organization to stress in your personal contacts and in your proposal.

Research your potential funder.

Before writing any proposal, much less submitting it, you need to develop a profile of the funder. This will include:

- The funder's stated areas of interest (and recent deviations);
- The types and sizes of grants awarded;
- Geographical and organizational preferences (and other giving limitations);
- Information on application guidelines; and
- A solid grasp of your organization's relationship with the funder, that is, Have you received past grants and were the projects successful?

Although harder to uncover, it will also help if you learn how the funder evaluates proposals. Is it by committee or by selected officials? Does your liaison within the funding organization have discretionary power with grants of certain amounts? And do laypeople or people trained in your field review proposals?

Speak to the funder's goals.

The funding source you're approaching has goals of its own. Too often organizations forget this and concern themselves only with what the grant will do for them and not what it could accomplish for the funder. But to successfully market your project, you can't emphasize *your* needs and *your* objectives alone. You must look at your project through the funder's eyes and determine how it will further their goals as you understand them.

Ask yourself, What exactly will the funder gain from making this grant? Is it healthier children? better schools? a safer world? Make the case. For even though your organization will carry out the project, the funder will share your achievement.

Call the funder before putting pen to paper.

To save yourself a lot of time you should—once you've identified a potential funder and before you start on any proposal—call them. You will, among other things, learn if there's a match between you, usually pick up some useful information, and get a sense of whether your project holds any interest for the funder.

Don't be coy over the phone. State why you're calling—to learn more about the funder and to ask if you can submit a proposal—and as briefly as you can, describe the project and the amount of money you need. Further, if you have a president or board member who can present your case persuasively, ask for an appointment. Although they are in the minority, some funders welcome personal visits.

If you get an appointment, make the most of it.

If you are in fact invited to the funder's office, it is a unique opportunity for which you should prepare thoroughly. First, give thought to who from your organization should attend the meeting. Usually it will be the CEO and a board member. Sometimes the project director might attend as well. Second, research the funder so that your team can demonstrate how the project will further the funder's goals. Third, make sure each team member has a role to play during the meeting. Finally, know before you walk through the door, just what it is you want to accomplish in the meeting.

Make sure your proposal has style and content.

The reality today is that your proposal will end up in a pile with literally hundreds of others. To have a fighting chance of being read, much less funded, it must be brief, concise, *and* compelling. But understand that's only a start. In addition to being highly readable, your proposal must also demonstrate that:

- Your project matches the funder's goals;
- It addresses an important need;
- You and your staff have the experience to carry out the project;
- Yours is a feasible approach to the problem;
- There will be a measurable outcome; and
- You're not duplicating the work of others.

Writing style is important but don't assume, like rookie proposal writers, that it ever overshadows content.

Blend logic and emotion in your writing.

Your proposal must present the facts as you see them, but this doesn't mean it should be devoid of emotion. In fact, you want to breathe life into your proposal, personalizing it with examples, anecdotes, and illustrations. Your aim is to *connect* so that the funder ends up sharing your vision.

To achieve this, take pains to:

- Write to a person, not to a funding organization;
- Stress the human side, how people's lives will be affected;
- Avoid the jargon that's part of the culture of every organization;
- Project confidence that the problem can be addressed; and
- Make your points directly, without paragraphs of build-up.

More important than any of these stylistic suggestions, however, is a character issue, namely, integrity. The goals you cite, the deadlines you set, the budget you present—all of these must be feasible and realistic. If you mislead a funder, not only will your reputation be stained, but word will rapidly spread that your organization should be avoided.

Write, don't fret.

As with most challenging tasks, when sitting down to draft a proposal, getting your pen to move can be the hardest part. You can make the writing easier, however, if you first approach the job in a casual way, jotting down answers to the following questions without worrying about the flow of your words.

- What's an appropriate name for this project?
- Why do we need to do it?
- What outcome do we hope to see?
- What means will we use to achieve the outcome?
- Who will be involved?
- What makes us qualified?
- In what time frame will we operate?
- How will we know if we succeed?
- How much will it cost?

Often it's best if the person who's most familiar with the project writes the first draft. After all, he or she will usually be its most informed advocate. If this isn't possible, the development officer can do the job after conferring with that individual.

Organize your proposal, paying careful attention to each component.

The individual components of your proposal will usually be the following:

A) Cover letter

Considering the sheer volume of proposals submitted, what you write in your cover letter may well determine whether your proposal is considered for review or rejected outright. This heavy burden makes it imperative that you be clear and succinct. In your cover letter:

- Explain your reasons for approaching this particular funder;
- Outline the contents of your proposal;
- Briefly describe the project;
- State how much you're seeking; and
- Mention that you'd be happy to meet with the funder and to provide additional information. Have the chairperson of your board or the CEO sign the letter.

B) Cover page

It may not happen frequently, but it's possible your cover letter will be separated from your proposal. If this happens, you want the funder to still be able to identify you, so include key information on your cover page such as your organization's name, address, telephone number, and contact person. It's also always helpful to personalize the cover page by incorporating the name of the funder (*A Proposal to the Halcyon Foundation for...*).

C) Table of contents

The table of contents is self-explanatory. It tells your reader what's included in the proposal and the order and page numbers of the items that appear. For clarity's sake, present the table on one full page.

D) Abstract

The abstract, or executive summary, distills the key information in your proposal into one or two pages. Write it after you've completed the rest of the proposal and include a statement of the problem, a description of the project including who will benefit and how, the amount of funding you need, and an explanation of how you will finance the project in the future.

Include as well a brief history of your organization and its mission. During the initial screening, your abstract may be the only part of your proposal read, so great care should be taken when composing it.

E) Statement of need

Your statement of need tells why your project is necessary. It presents facts and supporting evidence and attempts to show that your organization grasps the problem and is in a unique position to address it.

Additionally, your statement of need should document: the importance of addressing the problem not only to the people who will benefit, but also to society at large; the need to solve the problem at once; and how solving it matches the goals of the potential funding source.

F) Project description

This section, in which you describe the nuts and bolts of the project, usually has four parts:

- Objectives. Here you describe in detail the measurable outcomes you expect as well as the time frame in which these outcomes will be achieved.
- Methods. In this section, you chronicle the specific activities that will lead to achieving your objectives.
- Staffing and administration. Here you cite the staff, consultants, and volunteers who will be involved and their qualifications and specific roles. Also, you describe who will manage the project and how it will be done.
- Evaluation. Here you explain how you will evaluate the project, including the person who will head up the evaluation, how results will be reported, and who will receive copies of the evaluation.

G) Organization information

In this section, your aim is to build credibility for your organization. After all, credibility can be more important in securing the grant than your particular project.

Briefly describe how your organization came into being, your mission, and how the proposed project fits within that mission. Give details on the board and staff and their levels of expertise. Provide the names and backgrounds of those key to the project. And, to bolster your case, describe any special facilities or equipment you have to carry out the project.

H) Closing

This section serves as your closing argument, and you should make your case as compellingly as a prosecutor or defense attorney in court would. Summoning logic and emotion, restate what your organization wants to do and why it's important. Paint a picture of the people who will be served, and how they and society as a whole will benefit. Reemphasize how the project matches the funder's priorities. And, underscore why it must be done now.

I) Budget

Depending on the scope of the project, your budget may take up one page or six pages. It should outline the total cost of the undertaking and include items such as personnel costs, rental space, equipment, supplies, insurance, postage, and printing. Most important is that your budget be realistic and accurately reflect the size of your project. Here is also the place to explain how you will fund the project once this particular grant ends.

J) Appendices

Include in this section any supporting documents you feel will strengthen your case or are required by the funder, such as a fact sheet, a list of your governing board, case statement, annual report, previous grants received, biographical data on project participants, and your IRS tax exemption letter. Be thorough but don't of course overload the funder with peripheral material.

When only a simple letter is desired.

If yours is a small request, or if the funder dissuades full-blown proposals, a simple letter appeal may be appropriate. The elements of a letter proposal follow the format described earlier, just in shorter form.

In your three or four page letter, describe your project, the amount of funding you seek, the need for the project, the budget, what you hope to accomplish, and how you will evaluate the outcome. Include information about your organization and mission, your board of directors, and any pertinent material required by the funder.

Packaging your proposal.

Once you've prepared your proposal, you'll want to package it in the most effective way. Forego any fancy covers or binders (as these will be removed upon arrival anyway) and avoid embossing, gold leaf, and unusual paper. Keeping your presentation simple and tasteful will impress your potential funder more than any ornate dressings you might apply to it.

Follow up.

Don't put your feet on the desk once you've submitted your proposal. Instead, encourage your contacts to write letters or call or visit any of the funding officials they know.

Further, about two to four weeks after submitting the proposal, call to ask if additional information is required. Ask too if you can meet with the funder or arrange for a visit to your organization. Finally, just before the review meeting, call the funder again to ensure that your materials are complete.

If you receive a grant.

If you receive a grant, the obvious first thing to do is to send a thank-you letter (so obvious that many people forget to do it). Have your CEO or board president send out an official acknowledgment.

Secondly, ask the funder if you can publicize the grant. Often the funder encourages publicity but will want to review the text of your release.

Down the line you will be asked by the funding source to report on the results of your project. While some want updates quarterly or biannually, most request a final report several months after the project is completed. It is obviously to your advantage to comply promptly.

If your proposal is declined.

If your proposal is rejected, some funders will explain the reasons if you call, especially if you've had personal contact along the way. Others discourage follow-up calls, a frustrating behavior compounded when the funder's letter doesn't clarify why your project was rejected. Whatever reaction you receive, work hard to keep the lines of communication open. You will, by doing so, nurture the possibility of future funding.

Writing is only a part of developing a successful proposal, as this article has attempted to show. As important as the words you string together is the orderly, thorough, and thoughtful process that precedes putting pen to paper. Successful grant seeking is a culminating event and you will enjoy consistent success only if you view it in the total context described here.

FOUNDATIONS

ALABAMA

1
J.L. Bedsole Foundation
P.O. Box 1137
Mobile, AL 36633

Alabama High School of Mathematics and Science Foundation; Marine Environmental Sciences Consortium

Most grants awarded to organizations located in the Mobile vicinity.

2
Blount Foundation, Inc.
4520 Executive Park Drive
Montgomery, AL 36116
(205) 244-4348

College of Engineering; School of Mathematics and Sciences

Grants awarded to organizations located in areas of company operations (Blount, Inc.).

Typical grant range: $2,000 to $75,000

ALASKA

3
Z.J. Loussac Trust
c/o National Bank of Alaska
P.O. Box 100600
Anchorage, AK 99510
(907) 265-2841

Visually impaired (computer); performing arts (computer, copy machine); Public Radio (high-tech office equipment)

Most grants awarded to organizations located in the Anchorage vicinity.

Typical grant range: $1,000 to $7,000

4
Rasmuson Foundation
c/o National Bank of Alaska
P.O. Box 100600
Anchorage, AK 99510

Literacy project (computer); American Red Cross (computer); Very Special Arts (computer project); KUAC Radio and Television (computer)

Most grants awarded to organizations located in the Anchorage vicinity.

Typical grant range: $750 to $5,000

5
Skaggs Foundation
P.O. Box 20510
Juneau, AK 99802
(907) 463-4843

Prince William Sound Science Center; Alaska Discovery Foundation (computer)

Grants awarded to organizations located in Alaska.

Typical grant range: $1,000 to $6,000

ARIZONA

6
Flinn Foundation
3300 N. Central Avenue, Suite 2300
Phoenix, AZ 85012
(602) 274-9000

The Orme School (computer project for the library); University of Arizona Health Sciences Library and Area Health Education Centers (computers for the library)

Grants awarded to organizations located in Arizona.

Typical grant range: $5,000 to $150,000

7
Margaret T. Morris Foundation
P.O. Box 592
Prescott, AZ 86302
(602) 445-4010

Arizona Museum of Science and
Technology

Grants awarded to organizations located
in Arizona.

Typical grant range: $1,000 to $21,000

8
Research Corporation
101 North Wilmot Road, Suite 250
Tucson, AZ 85711
(602) 571-1111

Scientific research; higher education
(science)

Typical grant range: $10,000 to $40,000

9
Tucson Community Foundation
6601 E. Grant Road, Suite 111
Tucson, AZ 85715
(602) 722-1707

Visually impaired (computer training);
literacy program (computer project);
Amado Community Food Bank (copy
machine); Boys and Girls Clubs of Tucson
(Apple computers); Tucson Association
for Child Care (computer training for
teenage parents)

Most grants awarded to organizations
located in the Tucson vicinity.

ARKANSAS

10
Ross Foundation
1039 Henderson Street
Arkadelphia, AR 71923
(501) 246-9881

Higher education (computer network);
Arkadelphia Public Schools (computer,
mathematics and science departments);
Friends of the Museum (computer project)

Grants awarded to organizations located
in the Arkadelphia vicinity.

Typical grant range: $2,500 to $10,000

11
Walton Family Foundation, Inc.
125 West Central, Suite 217
Bentonville, AR 72712
(501) 273-5605

Bentonville Public Schools (computer)

Most grants awarded to organizations
located in Arkansas.

Typical grant range: $3,000 to $40,000

CALIFORNIA

12
Ahmanson Foundation
9215 Wilshire Blvd.
Beverly Hills, CA 90210
(310) 278-0770

Museum (computer); elementary school
(computer, software); higher education
(computer laboratory); Adult Skills Center
(high-tech office equipment); Youth Job
Awareness Project (computer)

Most grants awarded to organizations
located in the Los Angeles vicinity.

Typical grant range: $8,000 to $45,000

13
ARCO Foundation
515 S. Flower Street
Los Angeles, CA 90071
(213) 486-3342

Minorities (computer training); California
Academy of Mathematics and Science;
Boys and Girls Club (computer);
University of California, Los Angeles
(engineering program for minorities)

Grants awarded to organizations located
in areas of company operations (Atlantic
Richfield Co.).

14
Atkinson Foundation
1100 Grundy Lane, Suite 140
San Bruno, CA 94066
(415) 876-1359

Unified School District (computer training
workshop for teachers); St. Anthony's
Academy (high-tech office equipment)

Grants awarded to organizations located
in San Mateo County.

Typical grant range: $2,000 to $12,000

15
BankAmerica Foundation
Bank of America Center, Dept. 3246
P.O. Box 37000
San Francisco, CA 94137
(415) 953-3175

California Academy of Sciences; Cypress
College (computer); South Bay
Community Services Center (computer)

Grants awarded to organizations located
in areas of company operations
(BankAmerica Corp.).

Typical grant range: $1,000 to $15,000

16
Donald R. Barker Foundation, Inc.
P.O. Box 936
Rancho Mirage, CA 92270
(619) 324-2656

Boy Scouts of America (computer
project); American Diabetes Association
(computer)

Typical grant range: $2,000 to $11,000

17
**Arnold and Mabel Beckman
Foundation**
Grants Advisory Council
100 Academy Drive
Irvine, CA 92715
(714) 721-2222

California Institute of Technology
(scientific equipment)

Typical grant range: $100,000 to
$1,000,000

18
**H.N. and Frances C. Berger
Foundation**
P.O. Box 661178
Arcadia, CA 91066
(818) 447-3551

Whittier Union High School District
(electronic learning center); Foothill
Creative Arts Group (computer, software);
Los Angeles Urban League (computer);
City of Arcadia Public Library (compact
disk system); Pasadena City College
Foundation (computer for a high-tech
center that assists students with
disabilities)

Grants awarded to organizations located
in California.

Typical grant range: $10,000 to $100,000

19
Bothin Foundation
873 Sutter Street, Suite B
San Francisco, CA 94109
(415) 771-4300

Computer grants; high-tech office
equipment; disabled; health organizations;
cultural organizations

Typical grant range: $1,000 to $20,000

20

California Community Foundation
606 S. Olive Street, Suite 2400
Los Angeles, CA 90014
(213) 413-4042

Los Angeles Mission Foundation
(software)

Grants awarded to organizations located
in Los Angeles County.

Typical grant range: $3,000 to $30,000

21

**Community Foundation for Monterey
County**
P.O. Box 1384
Monterey, CA 93942
(408) 375-9712

Ventana Wilderness Sanctuary (copy
machine, computer); Goodwill Industries
(computer project); Alisal Union School
District (computer training for the
extended day program)

Grants awarded to organizations located
in Monterey County.

22

**Community Foundation of Santa Clara
County**
960 W. Hedding, Suite 220
San Jose, CA 95126
(408) 241-2666

Institute of Computer Technology; Tech
Museum of Innovation

Grants awarded to organizations located
in Santa Clara County.

Typical grant range: $2,000 to $10,000

23

Michael J. Connell Foundation
224 S. Lake Avenue, Suite 271
Pasadena, CA 91101

Computer Access Center

Most grants awarded to organizations
located in the Los Angeles vicinity.

Typical grant range: $10,000 to $50,000

24

Joseph Drown Foundation
1999 Ave. of the Stars, Suite 1930
Los Angeles, CA 90067
(310) 277-4488

Higher education (computer project for
the library); Museum of Science and
Industry; University Theatre and Radio
Station (high-tech office equipment);
California Neuropsychology Services
(computer laboratory)

Grants awarded to organizations located
in California.

Typical grant range: $10,000 to $75,000

25

East Bay Community Foundation
501 Wickson Avenue
Oakland, CA 94610
(510) 836-3223

Disabled Children's Computer Group

Grants awarded to organizations located
in Alameda and Contra Costa Counties.

Typical grant range: $500 to $10,000

26

Exchange Bank Foundation
c/o Exchange Bank
545 Fourth Street, P.O. Box 403
Santa Rosa, CA 95402
(707) 545-6220

Shelter (copy machine); Community
Resources for Independence (fax
machine); Hospital Chaplaincy Services
(laser printer)

Grants awarded to organizations located
in Sonoma County.

27
Freeman E. Fairfield Foundation
3610 Long Beach Blvd.
P.O. Box 7798
Long Beach, CA 90807
(310) 427-7219

Food Bank (fax machine); Long Beach
Council of Campfire (computer); Crippled
Children's Society (computer project)

Grants awarded to organizations located
in the Long Beach vicinity.

Typical grant range: $4,000 to $25,000

28
**First Interstate Bank of California
Foundation**
633 W. Fifth Street, T11-55
Los Angeles, CA 90071
(213) 614-3068

Central City Hospitality House
(computer)

Grants awarded to organizations located
in California.

Typical grant range: $2,000 to $30,000

29
Fleishhacker Foundation
c/o Christine Elbel
455 Market Street, Suite 1230
San Francisco, CA 94105
(415) 788-2909

San Francisco School of the Arts
(computer graphics laboratory)

Grants awarded to organizations located
in the San Francisco vicinity.

Typical grant range: $1,000 to $15,000

30
Fluor Foundation
3333 Michelson Drive
Irvine, CA 92730
(714) 975-6797

Higher education (engineering, science);
California State Polytechnic University
(School of Engineering)

Grants awarded to organizations located
in areas of company operations (Fluor
Corp.).

31
Foundation of the Litton Industries
360 N. Crescent Drive
Beverly Hills, CA 90210
(310) 859-5423

California Council on Science and
Technology; Stanford University (School
of Engineering)

Typical grant range: $1,000 to $20,000

32
**Georges and Germaine Fusenot
Charity Foundation**
7060 Hollywood Blvd., Suite 912
Hollywood, CA 90028
(213) 462-7702

Los Angeles Audubon Society (software)

Grants awarded to organizations located
in California.

33
Carl Gellert Foundation
2222 19th Avenue
San Francisco, CA 94116
(415) 566-4420

Elementary and secondary education
(computer grant, equipment for a science
project); higher education (engineering,
science laboratory); Early Childhood
Education Center (computer project for
children with disabilities)

Grants awarded to organizations located
in the San Francisco vicinity.

Typical grant range: $1,500 to $9,000

34
Walter and Elise Haas Fund
One Lombard Street, Suite 305
San Francisco, CA 94111
(415) 398-4474

Disabled Children's Computer Group;
Career Resources Development Center
(computer center)

Grants awarded to organizations located
in the San Francisco vicinity.

Typical grant range: $2,000 to $60,000

35
Harden Foundation
P.O. Box 779
Salinas, CA 93902
(408) 442-3005

Family Resource Center (computer);
American Cancer Society (fax machine);
Retired Volunteer Project (computer)

Grants awarded to organizations located
in the Salinas vicinity.

Typical grant range: $8,000 to $40,000

36
William and Flora Hewlett Foundation
525 Middlefield Road, Suite 200
Menlo Park, CA 94025
(415) 329-1070

Program for Appropriate Technology in
Health; University of California Press
(electronic publishing project)

Grants awarded to organizations located
in the San Francisco vicinity.

Typical grant range: $20,000 to $90,000

37
Humboldt Area Foundation
P.O. Box 99
Bayside, CA 95524
(707) 442-2993

Computer projects; high-tech office
equipment; elderly; disabled; youth
organizations; elementary school (science
equipment)

Grants awarded to organizations located
in Del Norte, Humboldt, Siskiyou, and
Trinity Counties.

Typical grant range: $1,000 to $11,000

38
James Irvine Foundation
One Market Plaza
Spear Tower, Suite 1715
San Francisco, CA 94105
(415) 777-2244

Museum (computer); Old Globe Theater
(computer)

Grants awarded to organizations located
in California.

Typical grant range: $20,000 to $100,000

39
William G. Irwin Charity Foundation
711 Russ Building
235 Montgomery Street
San Francisco, CA 94104
(415) 362-6954

Higher education (science laboratory);
California Historical Society (computer
project for the library); San Francisco
Opera (computer)

Typical grant range: $15,000 to $90,000

40
Jacobs Family Foundation, Inc.
P.O. Box 261519
San Diego, CA 92196
(619) 578-7256

Higher education (engineering); Pasadena
Neighborhood Housing Services
(software)

Typical grant range: $2,000 to $30,000

41
Fletcher Jones Foundation
One Wilshire Building, Suite 1210
624 S. Grand Avenue
Los Angeles, CA 90017
(213) 689-9292

Harvey Mudd College (computer); John
Tracy Clinic (computer); Psoriasis
Research Foundation (computer); Library
Foundation of Los Angeles (computer);
World Opportunities International
(computer)

Grants awarded to organizations located
in California.

Typical grant range: $12,000 to $165,000

42
W.M. Keck Foundation
555 S. Flower Street, Suite 3230
Los Angeles, CA 90071
(213) 680-3833

Higher education (computer science,
mathematics, science, scientific
equipment); Archdiocese of Los Angeles
(computer project)

Typical grant range: $150,000 to $700,000

43
Louis R. Lurie Foundation
555 California Street, Suite 5100
San Francisco, CA 94104
(415) 392-2470

Museum of Science and Industry;
Achievement Awards for College
Scientists

Typical grant range: $5,000 to $30,000

44
Miranda Lux Foundation
57 Post Street, Suite 510
San Francisco, CA 94104
(415) 981-2966

Youth Guidance Center (computer literacy
program); Mercy High School (upgrade
computer, video equipment); St. Emydius
School (computer); Accion Latino
(computer); Career Resource
Development Center (computer)

Grants awarded to organizations located
in San Francisco.

Typical grant range: $1,000 to $20,000

45
Bertha Russ Lytel Foundation
P.O. Box 893
Ferndale, CA 95536

Elementary school (computer); Police
Department (communications equipment);
Adult Day Health Care (copy machine);
Redwood Family Institute (computer,
copy machine); Youth Education Services
(copy machine); Ferndale Union High
School (computers)

Grants awarded to organizations located
in Humboldt County.

Typical grant range: $500 to $25,000

46
Marin Community Foundation
17 E. Sir Francis Drake Blvd., Suite 200
Larkspur, CA 94939
(415) 461-3333

Marin County Library (computer);
Environmental Defense Fund (computer
project); CompuMentor Project (computer
project for housing program); San Rafael
City Schools in Partnership with Lucas
Arts (computer project)

Grants awarded to organizations located
in Marin County.

Typical grant range: $5,000 to $200,000

47
McConnell Foundation
P.O. Box 991870
Redding, CA 96099
(916) 222-0696

Science Museum (computer project);
National Park Service (computer,
software); Tule Lake High School
(computer project for the science
department)

Typical grant range: $3,000 to $80,000

48
McKesson Foundation, Inc.
One Post Street
San Francisco, CA 94104
(415) 983-8673

Computer projects; social service
organizations; computer training for
nonprofit organizations

Grants awarded to organizations located
in the San Francisco vicinity.

Typical grant range: $1,000 to $20,000

49
David and Lucile Packard Foundation
300 Second Street, Suite 200
Los Altos, CA 94022
(415) 948-7658

Higher education (science, mathematics, engineering, computer science); The Scientific Research Society; Tech Museum of Innovation

Most grants awarded to organizations located in Monterey, San Mateo, Santa Clara, and Santa Cruz Counties.

Typical grant range: $5,000 to $100,000

50
Ralph M. Parsons Foundation
1055 Wilshire Blvd., Suite 1701
Los Angeles, CA 90017
(213) 482-3185

Computer grants; software grants; disabled; elderly; scientific equipment; higher education (engineering, science, mathematics); Claremont University Center and Graduate School (computer)

Most grants awarded to organizations located in Los Angeles County.

Typical grant range: $15,000 to $85,000

51
Pasadena Foundation
16 N. Marengo Avenue, Suite 302
Pasadena, CA 91101
(818) 796-2097

Council on Alcoholism (copy machine); Nature Center (computer, software, printer); Girl Scouts (modems, fax machine); Child S.H.A.R.E. (computer, printer); Hospice of Pasadena (laser printer); Pasadena Educational Foundation (computer); Pasadena Historical Society (computer, software); Mental Health Association (copy machine)

Grants awarded to organizations located in the Pasadena vicinity.

Typical grant range: $1,500 to $30,000

52
Plum Foundation
P.O. Box 1613
Studio City, CA 91604
(818) 766-8064

Westside Arts Center (computer)

Typical grant range: $5,000 to $30,000

53
Sacramento Regional Foundation
2180 Harvard Street, Suite 255
Sacramento, CA 95815
(916) 927-2241

Planned Parenthood (computer project)

Grants awarded in the following counties: El Dorado, Placer, Sacramento, and Yolo.

Typical grant range: $500 to $9,000

54
San Diego Community Foundation
Wells Fargo Bank Building
101 W. Broadway, Suite 1120
San Diego, CA 92101
(619) 239-8815

San Diego Space and Science Foundation; San Diego Rescue Mission (computer)

Grants awarded to organizations located in San Diego County.

Typical grant range: $1,000 to $15,000

55
San Francisco Foundation
685 Market Street, Suite 910
San Francisco, CA 94105
(415) 495-3100

California Academy of Sciences; Options for Women Over Forty (computer training)

Grants awarded in Alameda, Contra Costa, Marin, San Francisco, and San Mateo Counties.

Typical grant range: $2,000 to $40,000

56
Santa Barbara Foundation
15 E. Carrillo Street
Santa Barbara, CA 93101
(805) 963-1873

Santa Barbara Rape Crisis Center (copy machine); Dyslexia Awareness and Resource Center (computer, software, printer); Alzheimer's Disease and Related Disorders Association (copy machine); Arts Outreach (computer, fax machine)

Grants awarded to organizations located in Santa Barbara County.

Typical grant range: $5,000 to $25,000

57
Sega Youth Education & Health Foundation
255 Shoreline Drive, Suite 200
Redwood City, CA 94065

Technology Resources for Elementary Education; Hillsdale High School (computer); Disabled Children's Computer Group (computer)

58
Sierra Health Foundation
1321 Garden Highway
Sacramento, CA 95833
(916) 922-4755

Health Center (computer); Nonprofit Resource Center (computer project)

Typical grant range: $15,000 to $50,000

59
May and Stanley Smith Trust
49 Geary Street, Suite 244
San Francisco, CA 94108
(415) 391-0292

Disabled Children's Computer Group; Rescue Mission of Richmond (computer)

Most grants awarded to organizations located in the San Francisco vicinity.

Typical grant range: $1,500 to $6,000

60
James L. Stamps Foundation, Inc.
P.O. Box 250
Downey, CA 90241
(310) 861-3112

First Baptist Church (computer project); Heart Impact Ministries (software); Community Church (copy machine, laser printer); Wycliffe Bible Translators (computer)

61
John Stauffer Charitable Trust
301 N. Lake Avenue, 10th Floor
Pasadena, CA 91101
(818) 793-9400

University of California (scientific equipment); University of Redlands (science project); California Institute of Technology (computer graphic project); Saint John's Hospital and Health Center (computer)

Grants awarded to organizations located in California.

Typical grant range: $30,000 to $120,000

62
Harry and Grace Steele Foundation
441 Old Newport Blvd., Suite 301
Newport Beach, CA 92663
(714) 631-9158

Planned Parenthood (computer)

Grants awarded to organizations located in Orange County.

Typical grant range: $10,000 to $125,000

63
Glen and Dorothy Stillwell Charitable Trust
301 N. Lake Avenue, 10th Floor
Pasadena, CA 91101
(818) 793-9400

Computer grants; high-tech equipment; disabled; child welfare; social welfare

Grants awarded to organizations located in Orange County.

Typical grant range: $7,000 to $12,000

64
Toyota USA Foundation
19001 S. Western Avenue
Torrance, CA 90509
(310) 618-6766

Animal welfare (computer); Museum of Science; University of California, Berkeley (workshop for science and mathematics teachers in rural schools)

Typical grant range: $10,000 to $75,000

65
Alice Tweed Tuohy Foundation
205 E. Carrillo Street, Room 219
Santa Barbara, CA 93101
(805) 962-6430

Foundation for City College (computer training); Sansum Medical Research (computer, software)

Grants awarded to organizations located in the Santa Barbara vicinity.

Typical grant range: $1,000 to $15,000

66
Unocal Foundation
1201 W. Fifth Street
Los Angeles, CA 90017
(213) 977-6877

Higher education (petroleum engineering, chemistry); California Academy of Mathematics and Science; California State University at Fullerton (engineering, computer science)

Typical grant range: $2,000 to $30,000

67
Valley Foundation
P.O. Box 5129
San Jose, CA 95150
(408) 292-1124

Tech Museum of Innovation; Planned Parenthood (computer); Evergreen Valley College (software for the Nursing Department)

Grants awarded to organizations located in Santa Clara County.

Typical grant range: $15,000 to $85,000

68
Ventura County Community Foundation
1355 Del Norte Road
Camarillo, CA 93010
(805) 988-0196

Boys and Girls Club (computer training); Catholic Charities (computer); Visiting Nurse Association (computer)

Grants awarded to organizations located in Ventura County.

Typical grant range: $500 to $7,000

69
Weingart Foundation
1055 W. Seventh Street, Suite 3050
Los Angeles, CA 90017
(213) 688-7799

Secondary education (computer laboratory, science laboratory); Mayfield Junior School of the Holy Child Jesus (library automation)

Grants awarded to organizations located in southern California.

Typical grant range: $5,000 to $150,000

70
L.K. Whittier Foundation
1260 Huntington Drive, Suite 204
South Pasadena, CA 91030

Higher education (science scholarships); school district (computer laboratory); Braille Institute Auxiliary (computer laboratory)

Most grants awarded to preselected organizations.

Most grants awarded to organizations located in Los Angeles.

Typical grant range: $2,000 to $35,000

COLORADO

71
Boettcher Foundation
600 17th Street, Suite 2210 South
Denver, CO 80202
(303) 534-1937

Higher education (building funds for the science department); Colorado Minority Engineering Association

Grants awarded to organizations located in Colorado.

Typical grant range: $5,000 to $45,000

72
Collins Foundation
c/o Norwest Bank, Boulder, N.A.
P.O. Box 299
Boulder, CO 80306
(303) 441-0310

Health organization (high-tech office equipment); YWCA (computer)

Grants awarded to organizations located in Boulder County.

Typical grant range: $500 to $3,500

73
Adolph Coors Foundation
3773 Cherry Creek North Drive, Suite 955
Denver, CO 80209
(303) 388-1636

Higher education (computer for the college library); disabled (software)

Grants awarded to organizations located in Colorado.

Typical grant range: $5,000 to $45,000

74
Denver Foundation
455 Sherman Street, Suite 220
Denver, CO 80203
(303) 778-7587

Very Special Arts (computer); Boulder County Hospice (computer, software)

Typical grant range: $2,000 to $20,000

75
El Pomar Foundation
Ten Lake Circle
Colorado Springs, CO 80906
(719) 633-7733

Historic Denver (computer, software); United States Association for Blind Athletes (computer, software); Children's Museum of Denver (Science Center)

Grants awarded to organizations located in Colorado.

Typical grant range: $3,000 to $50,000

76
Gates Foundation
3200 Cherry Creek South Drive, Suite 630
Denver, CO 80209
(303) 722-1881

Colorado Alliance for Science; Colorado Minority Engineering Association; Country Day School (building funds for the science department)

Grants awarded to organizations located in Colorado.

Typical grant range: $5,000 to $30,000

77
Helen K. and Arthur E. Johnson Foundation
1700 Broadway, Room 2302
Denver, CO 80290
(303) 861-4127

Lutheran High School (computers)

Grants awarded to organizations located in Colorado.

Typical grant range: $12,000 to $100,000

78
US WEST Foundation
7800 E. Orchard Road, Suite 300
Englewood, CO 80111
(303) 793-6648

Community college (computer for multimedia lab); American Indian Science and Engineering Society; Metro Crisis Intervention Service (computer)

Grants awarded to organizations located in areas of company operations (US WEST).

Typical grant range: $3,000 to $20,000

CONNECTICUT

79
Community Foundation of Southeastern Connecticut
302 State Street
P.O. Box 769
New London, CT 06320
(203) 442-3572

The Center: A Drop-In Learning and Resource Center (computer, printer, fax machine); Connecticut Early Music Festival (printer); Jewish Family Services (computer, software, printer)

Grants awarded to organizations located in southeastern Connecticut.

80
Charles E. Culpeper Foundation, Inc.
Financial Centre
695 E. Main Street, Suite 404
Stamford, CT 06901
(203) 975-1240

Computer grants; cultural organizations; disabled; minorities; Public Library (computer project)

Typical grant range: $3,000 to $55,000

81
Educational Foundation of America
35 Church Lane
Westport, CT 06880
(203) 226-6498

American Indian Science and Engineering Society; Institute of Computer Application for the Learning Disabled; Texas Scottish Rite Hospital for Crippled Children (computer, software)

Typical grant range: $10,000 to $75,000

82
Sherman Fairchild Foundation, Inc.
71 Arch Street
Greenwich, CT 06830
(203) 661-9360

Higher education (science, engineering, scientific equipment); Hotchkiss School (science laboratory equipment)

Typical grant range: $50,000 to $500,000

83
GTE Foundation
One Stamford Forum
Stamford, CT 06904
(203) 965-3620

Higher education (computer science, engineering, minorities); Museum of Science and Industry

Grants awarded to organizations located in areas of company operations (GTE Corp.).

Typical grant range: $1,000 to $25,000

84
Hartford Foundation for Public Giving
85 Gillett Street
Hartford, CT 06105
(203) 548-1888

Greater Hartford Arts Council (computer);
Urban League (computer project);
Hartford Symphony Orchestra
(computer); American Red Cross
(computer); Greater Hartford Community
College Foundation (computer project for
the nursing department)

Grants awarded to organizations located
in the Hartford vicinity.

Typical grant range: $25,000 to $50,000

85
Olin Corporation Charitable Trust
501 Merritt Seven
P.O. Box 4500
Norwalk, CT 06856
(203) 750-3000

Higher education (engineering, science);
Future Scientists Foundation

Grants awarded to organizations located
in areas of company operations (Olin
Corporation).

86
Stanley Works Foundation
1000 Stanley Drive
New Britain, CT 06053
(203) 225-5111

Higher education (engineering, science);
Connecticut Pre-Engineering Program

Grants awarded to organizations located
in areas of company operations (The
Stanley Works).

Typical grant range: $1,000 to $50,000

87
Union Carbide Foundation, Inc.
39 Old Ridgebury Road
Danbury, CT 06817
(203) 794-6942

Elementary and secondary education
(science, mathematics); National Action
Council for Minorities in Engineering;
National Youth Science Camp

Grants awarded to organizations located
in areas of company operations (Union
Carbide Corporation).

88
Waterbury Foundation
156 W. Main Street
Waterbury, CT 06702
(203) 753-1315

Computers 4 Kids

Grants awarded to organizations located
in the Waterbury vicinity.

Typical grant range: $2,500 to $45,000

DELAWARE

89
Chichester duPont Foundation, Inc.
3120 Kennett Pike
Wilmington, DE 19807
(302) 658-5244

Silver Creek Alternative School
(computer); Walker Center (computer)

Typical grant range: $10,000 to $44,000

90
Crestlea Foundation, Inc.
1004 Wilmington Trust Center
Wilmington, DE 19801
(302) 654-2489

United Methodist Home (computer);
United Cerebral Palsy (computer);
American Cancer Society (printer)

Grants awarded to organizations located
in Delaware.

Typical grant range: $1,000 to $20,000

91

Crystal Trust
1088 DuPont Building
Wilmington, DE 19898
(302) 774-8421

Westside Health Services (computer);
Delaware Hospice (computer); Leukemia
Society of America (computer); National
Society of Fund Raising Executives
(computer); Delaware Technical and
Community College (computer project for
the library)

Grants awarded to organizations located
in Delaware, with an emphasis in
Wilmington.

Typical grant range: $5,000 to $75,000

92

Laffey-McHugh Foundation
1220 Market Building
P.O. Box 2207
Wilmington, DE 19899
(302) 658-9141

Delaware Technical and Community
College (computer); Holy Angel School
(three computers); Recording for the
Blind (electronic textbooks)

Grants awarded to organizations located
in Delaware, with an emphasis in
Wilmington.

Typical grant range: $4,000 to $40,000

93

Longwood Foundation, Inc.
1004 Wilmington Trust Center
Wilmington, DE 19801
(302) 654-2477

Museum (computer); Public Library
(computer project); Meals on Wheels
(computer, software)

Grants awarded to organizations located
in Delaware, with an emphasis in
Wilmington.

Typical grant range: $20,000 to $325,000

94

**Raskob Foundation for Catholic
Activities, Inc.**
P.O. Box 4019
Wilmington, DE 19807
(302) 655-4440

Computer grants; software grants;
social welfare; secondary education
(mathematics, science, computer
department); higher education (computer
project for the library)

Most grants awarded to Roman Catholic
organizations.

Typical grant range: $3,000 to $15,000

95

Welfare Foundation, Inc.
1004 Wilmington Trust Center
Wilmington, DE 19801
(302) 654-2489

Public Television (computer); Newark
Day Nursery Association (computer)

Grants awarded to organizations located
in Delaware, with an emphasis in
Wilmington.

Typical grant range: $10,000 to $60,000

DISTRICT OF COLUMBIA

96

**Morris and Gwendolyn Cafritz
Foundation**
1825 K Street, N.W., 14th Floor
Washington, DC 20006
(202) 223-3100

Learning disabled (computer training);
Carnegie Institution of Washington, DC
(science department); Council for Basic
Education (program for teaching
mathematics in elementary schools)

Grants awarded to organizations located
in the Washington, DC vicinity.

Typical grant range: $15,000 to $60,000

97

Dole Foundation for Employment of People with Disabilities
1819 H Street, N.W., Suite 340
Washington, DC 20006
(202) 457-0318

Center for Computer Assistance for the Disabled (computer training for people with disabilities)

Typical grant range: $1,000 to $25,000

98

John Edward Fowler Memorial Foundation
1725 K Street, N.W., Suite 1201
Washington, DC 20006
(202) 728-9080

Community Family Life Services (computer)

Grants awarded to organizations located in the Washington, DC vicinity.

Typical grant range: $4,000 to $15,000

99

Mary and Daniel Loughran Foundation, Inc.
c/o Security Trust Co., N.A.
15th Street and Pennsylvania Ave., N.W.
Washington, DC 20013
(202) 624-5744

Stone Ridge Country Day School of the Sacred Heart (computer center); Theological Seminary (computer)

Typical grant range: $5,000 to $20,000

100

MCI Foundation
1801 Pennsylvania Ave., N.W.
Washington, DC 20006
(202) 887-2106

Higher education (computer science, mathematics, science); Electronic Frontier Foundation; Boys and Girls Clubs (computer training)

Typical grant range: $1,000 to $20,000

101

Eugene and Agnes E. Meyer Foundation
1400 16th Street, N.W., Suite 360
Washington, DC 20036
(202) 483-8294

Olney Theatre Corporation (computerized lighting system); Ministry of Montgomery County (computer project)

Grants awarded to organizations located in the Washington, DC vicinity.

Typical grant range: $12,000 to $35,000

102

Mitsubishi Electric America Foundation
1150 Connecticut Ave., N.W., Suite 1020
Washington, DC 20036
(202) 857-0031

Special Education Technical Resource Center (software)

Most grants awarded to organizations located in areas of company operations (Mitsubishi Electric Corp.).

Typical grant range: $5,000 to $25,000

103

Hattie M. Strong Foundation
1620 I Street, N.W., Suite 700
Washington, DC 20006
(203) 331-1619

Chelsea School (computer training for children with learning disabilities using laptop computers)

Most grants awarded to organizations located in the Washington, DC vicinity.

Typical grant range: $1,000 to $5,000

FLORIDA

104
Cordelia Lee Beattie Foundation Trust
1800 Second Street, Suite 905
Sarasota, FL 34236
(813) 957-0442

Sarasota County Arts Council (computer, software); School Board of Sarasota County (video switcher)

Grants awarded to organizations located in Sarasota County.

Typical grant range: $2,000 to $15,000

105
Broward Community Foundation, Inc.
800 E. Broward Blvd., Suite 610
Ft. Lauderdale, FL 33301
(954) 761-9503

Physically disabled (computer project); literacy program (computer project); museum (computer); Public Library (computer); Insight for the Blind (computer)

Grants awarded to organizations located in Broward County.

Typical grant range: $2,000 to $6,000

106
Edyth Bush Charitable Foundation, Inc.
199 E. Welbourne Avenue
P.O. Box 1967
Winter Park, FL 32790
(407) 647-4322

Computer grants; software; high-tech office equipment; health organizations; youth organizations; Embry-Riddle Aeronautical University (computer laboratory equipment)

Most grants awarded to organizations located within a 100 mile distance from Winter Park.

Typical grant range: $10,000 to $60,000

107
Community Foundation for Palm Beach and Martin Counties, Inc.
324 Datura Street, Suite 340
West Palm Beach, FL 33401
(407) 659-6800

Palm Beach Marine Institute (computer); Historical Society of Palm Beach (computer project); Hobe Sound Elementary School (science project)

Grants awarded to organizations located in Palm Beach, Martin, and Hendry Counties.

Typical grant range: $1,000 to $12,000

108
Community Foundation of Collier County
4949 Tamiami Trail North, Suite 202
Naples, FL 33940
(813) 649-5000

Health organizations (audio-visual equipment); Immokalee Friendship Center (computer); Naples Civil Air Patrol (communication equipment)

Grants awarded to organizations located in Collier County.

109
Community Foundation of Greater Tampa, Inc.
315 E. Madison, Suite 600
Tampa, FL 33602
(813) 221-1776

High school (science department); West Shore Elementary School (computer laboratory)

Grants awarded to organizations located in the Tampa vicinity.

Typical grant range: $1,500 to $5,000

110

Community Foundation of Sarasota County, Inc.
P.O. Box 49587
Sarasota, FL 34230
(813) 955-3000

Computer grants; health organizations; social welfare

Grants awarded to organizations located in Sarasota County.

Typical grant range: $500 to $5,000

111

Conn Memorial Foundation, Inc.
5401 W. Kennedy Blvd., Suite 530
Tampa, FL 33609
(813) 282-4922

Computer grants; social welfare; disabled

Grants awarded to organizations located in Hillsborough and Pinellas Counties.

Typical grant range: $2,000 to $20,000

112

Arthur Vining Davis Foundations
111 Riverside Avenue, Suite 130
Jacksonville, FL 32202
(904) 359-0670

Higher education (computer; high-tech equipment for the library); Jacksonville University (scientific laboratory); National Science Center Foundation (mathematics research project); Episcopal Theological Seminary (library automation)

Typical grant range: $35,000 to $150,000

113

Jessie Ball duPont Fund
225 Water Street, Suite 1200
Jacksonville, FL 32202
(904) 353-0890

Saint Elizabeth's Church and Minister's Discretionary Fund (computer project); Stetson University (computer project for the library); United Way (computer project)

Only previous grant recipients from this foundation are eligible to apply for another grant.

Typical grant range: $5,000 to $85,000

114

Charles A. Frueauff Foundation, Inc.
307 E. Seventh Avenue
Tallahassee, FL 32303
(904) 561-3508

Higher education (automate library, science department); Young Scientists Education Fund

Typical grant range: $10,000 to $35,000

115

John S. and James L. Knight Foundation
One Biscayne Tower, Suite 3800
Two S. Biscayne Boulevard
Miami, FL 33131
(305) 539-0009

Museum (high-tech project for digital cataloging); Computer Access Center (for preschool children with disabilities); American Woman's Economic Development Corp. (computer); United Way (computer, software); Rape Crisis Center (computer)

Typical grant range: $10,000 to $125,000

116
John E. & Aliese Price Foundation, Inc.
1279 Lavin Lane
North Fort Myers, FL 33917
(813) 656-0196

Florida Engineering Society Foundation;
Math, Science and Technology
Foundation

Most grants awarded to organizations
located in the Fort Myers vicinity.

Typical grant range: $500 to $8,000

117
**Paul E. & Klare N. Reinhold
Foundation, Inc.**
225 Water Street, Suite 2175
Jacksonville, FL 32202
(904) 354-2359

Marine Institute (two Apple computers)

Typical grant range: $1,000 to $20,000

118
**William G. Selby and Marie Selby
Foundation**
1800 Second Street, Suite 905
Sarasota, FL 34236
(813) 957-0442

Computer grants; software; social welfare;
health organizations; youth organizations;
Sarasota County School System
(computer, software)

Typical grant range: $5,000 to $45,000

119
**Southwest Florida Community
Foundation, Inc.**
P.O. Box 9326
Fort Myers, FL 33902
(813) 334-0377

Middle school (science project); high
school (computer laboratory); community
college (computer laboratory)

Grants awarded to organizations located
in southwest Florida.

Typical grant range: $3,000 to $12,000

120
**Hugh and Mary Wilson
Foundation, Inc.**
7188 Beneva Road
Sarasota, FL 34238
(813) 921-2856

United Way (computer); Vocational Tech
Center (computer)

Typical grant range: $1,000 to $20,000

GEORGIA

121
Peyton Anderson Foundation, Inc.
1408 Charter Medical Building
Macon, GA 31201
(912) 743-5359

Bibb County Board of Education
(technology program)

Most grants awarded to organizations
located in the Macon vicinity.

122
BellSouth Foundation
c/o BellSouth Corporation
1155 Peachtree Street, N.E., Room 7H08
Atlanta, GA 30309
(404) 249-2396

Higher education (engineering
department); Educational Technology
Cooperative Program; County Public
School (computer project)

Grants awarded to organizations located
in areas of company operations (BellSouth
Corp.).

Typical grant range: $15,000 to $300,000

123
J. Bulow Campbell Foundation
1530 Trust Co. Tower
25 Park Place, N.E.
Atlanta, GA 30303
(404) 658-9066

Salvation Army (computer project); Big
Brothers/Big Sisters (computer);
Westminster Schools (science department)

Most grants awarded to organizations
located in Georgia.

Typical grant range: $75,000 to $400,000

124
Lettie Pate Evans Foundation, Inc.
50 Hurt Plaza, Suite 1200
Atlanta, GA 30303
(404) 522-6755

National Science Center Foundation;
Wesleyan College (computer for the
library)

Grants awarded to organizations located
in the Atlanta vicinity.

Typical grant range: $75,000 to $300,000

125
Georgia Power Foundation, Inc.
333 Piedmont Avenue, 20th Floor
Atlanta, GA 30308
(404) 526-6784

Science and Technology Museum;
Georgia Youth and Technology Center

Grants awarded to organizations located
in Georgia.

Typical grant range: $2,000 to $25,000

126
**Metropolitan Atlanta Community
Foundation, Inc.**
The Hurt Building, Suite 449
Atlanta, GA 30303
(404) 688-5525

Atlanta Community Food Bank (software)

Grants awarded to organizations located
in the Atlanta vicinity.

Typical grant range: $2,000 to $15,000

127
James Hyde Porter Testamentary Trust
Trust Co. Bank of Middle Georgia, N.A.
606 Cherry Street, P.O. Box 4248
Macon, GA 31208
(912) 755-5164

Middle school (software for a writing
laboratory); Foundation for Speech and
Hearing (computer)

Grants awarded to organizations located
in Bibb and Newton Counties.

Typical grant range: $5,000 to $25,000

128
Joseph B. Whitehead Foundation
50 Hurt Plaza, Suite 1200
Atlanta, GA 30303
(404) 522-6755

Fernbank Science Center; Arthritis
Foundation (computer)

Grants awarded to organizations located
in the Atlanta vicinity.

Typical grant range: $50,000 to $400,000

129
Robert W. Woodruff Foundation, Inc.
50 Hurt Plaza, Suite 1200
Atlanta, GA 30303
(404) 522-6755

Education Center for Science and
Technology; Robert W. Woodruff Library
(automate library)

Grants awarded to organizations located
in Atlanta.

Typical grant range: $50,000 to $1,500,000

HAWAII

130
Atherton Family Foundation
c/o Hawaiian Trust Co., Ltd.
P.O. Box 3170
Honolulu, HI 96802
(808) 537-6333

Maui AIDS Foundation (computer);
Hawaii Council on Economic Education
(computer); Hawaiian Humane Society
(software); West Hawaii Arts Guild (copy
machine)

Grants awarded to organizations located
in Hawaii.

Typical grant range: $2,000 to $20,000

131
Samuel N. and Mary Castle Foundation
900 Fort Street Mall, Suite 1300
Honolulu, HI 96813
(808) 537-6333

Hawaii Opera Theatre (wireless
communication equipment)

Grants awarded to organizations located
in Hawaii.

Typical grant range: $2,500 to $20,000

132
Cooke Foundation, Limited
c/o Hawaiian Trust Co., Ltd.
P.O. Box 3170
Honolulu, HI 96802
(808) 537-6333

Hawaii International Film Festival
(computer); Culture and Arts Society
(computer)

Grants awarded to organizations located
in Hawaii.

Typical grant range: $2,000 to $15,000

133
Hawaii Community Foundation
900 Fort Street Mall, Suite 1300
Honolulu, HI 96813
(808) 537-6333

Elderly (computer project); legal clinic
(computer, software, printer); Girl Scout
Council (fax machine); YMCA (fax
machine); Honolulu Symphony Society
(computer); Botanical Garden (computer
project)

Grants awarded to organizations located
in Hawaii.

Typical grant range: $3,000 to $40,000

134
McInerny Foundation
c/o Hawaiian Trust Co., Ltd.
130 Merchant Street
Honolulu, HI 96813
(808) 538-4944

Computer grants; high-tech office
equipment; social welfare; disabled;
cultural organizations

Grants awarded to organizations located
in Hawaii.

Typical grant range: $5,000 to $20,000

135
**Bernice and Conrad Von Hamm
Foundation**
c/o Hawaiian Trust Co., Ltd.
P.O. Box 3170
Honolulu, HI 96802

Girl Scout Council of Hawaii (computer)

Grants awarded to organizations located
in Hawaii.

136
Elsie H. Wilcox Foundation
c/o Hawaiian Trust Co., Ltd.
P.O. Box 3170
Honolulu, HI 96802

Island School (computer)

137

G.N. Wilcox Trust
c/o Hawaiian Trust Co., Ltd.
P.O. Box 3170
Honolulu, HI 96802
(808) 538-4944

March of Dimes (computer project);
Goodwill Industries (computer); Waikiki
Community Center (computer, printer)

Typical grant range: $1,000 to $7,500

IDAHO

138

Leland D. Beckman Foundation
c/o Holden, Kidwell, Hahn & Crapo
P.O. Box 50130
Idaho Falls, ID 83405

Family Assistance Transitional Housing
(computer, software); Idaho Falls Public
Library (Internet access project); Salman
Jr. High School (computer, software)

Grants awarded to organizations located
in Idaho Falls.

Typical grant range: $1,000 to $8,000

139

Idaho Community Foundation
101 S. Capitol Blvd., Suite 1001
Boise, ID 83702
(208) 342-3535

Literacy Lab (computer, software,
computer training); Wallace District
Mining Museum (video equipment);
Aberdeen Education Foundation (upgrade
computer at an elementary school)

Grants awarded to organizations located
in Idaho.

Typical grant range: $500 to $5,000

140

**Claude R. and Ethel B. Whittenberger
Foundation**
P.O. Box 1073
Caldwell, ID 83606
(208) 459-0091

Public Library (computer)

Grants awarded to organizations located
in Idaho.

Typical grant range: $1,000 to $9,000

ILLINOIS

141

Abbott Laboratories Fund
Dept. 379, Building 6C
One Abbott Park Road
North Chicago, IL 60064
(708) 937-7075

Museum of Science and Industry;
Northwestern University (engineering,
physical sciences)

Grants awarded to organizations located
in areas of company operations (Abbott
Laboratories).

Typical grant range: $1,000 to $20,000

142

Ameritech Foundation
30 S. Wacker Drive, 34th Floor
Chicago, IL 60606

National Action Council for Minorities in
Engineering; Illinois Mathematics and
Science Academy; Museum of Science
and Industry; Corporation for Educational
Technology; United Cerebral Palsy
(technology center)

Grants awarded to organizations located
in the Great Lakes region.

Typical grant range: $5,000 to $60,000

143

Beloit Foundation, Inc.
11722 Main Street
Roscoe, IL 61073
(815) 623-6600

United Way (computer)

Typical grant range: $2,000 to $40,000

144
Blowitz-Ridgeway Foundation
1 Northfield Plaza, Suite 230
Northfield, IL 60093
(847) 446-1010

Disabled (computer project); computer training for nonprofit organizations

Grants awarded to organizations located in Illinois.

Typical grant range: $2,000 to $25,000

145
Buchanan Family Foundation
222 E. Wisconsin Avenue
Lake Forest, IL 60045

Chicago Academy of Sciences; Museum of Science and Industry

Most grants awarded to organizations located in the Chicago vicinity.

Typical grant range: $10,000 to $50,000

146
Chicago Community Trust
222 N. LaSalle Street, Suite 1400
Chicago, IL 60601
(312) 372-3356

Community development (computer project); Council for Jewish Elderly (computer, software)

Grants awarded to organizations located in the Chicago vicinity.

Typical grant range: $15,000 to $70,000

147
Chicago Tribune Foundation
435 N. Michigan Avenue
Chicago, IL 60611
(312) 222-4300

Museum of Science and Industry; Urban League of Chicago (computer project)

Most grants awarded to organizations located in the Chicago vicinity.

Typical grant range: $5,000 to $20,000

148
Henry P. Crowell and Susan C. Crowell Trust
Lock Box 442
Chicago, IL 60690
(312) 372-5202

School of the Bible (computer); College of the Bible (software)

Typical grant range: $5,000 to $30,000

149
Doris and Victor Day Foundation, Inc.
1705 Second Avenue, Suite 424
Rock Island, IL 61201
(309) 788-2300

Bethany Home (computer); Illinois Migrant Council (computer, printer)

Grants awarded to organizations located in the Illinois/Iowa Quad Cities.

Typical grant range: $1,000 to $15,000

150
Field Foundation of Illinois, Inc.
200 S. Wacker Drive, #4
Chicago, IL 60606
(312) 263-3211

Computer training for nonprofit organizations

Grants awarded to organizations located in the Chicago vicinity.

Typical grant range: $5,000 to $45,000

151
Lloyd A. Fry Foundation
135 S. LaSalle Street, Suite 1910
Chicago, IL 60603
(312) 580-0310

Higher education (science, mathematics); Museum of Science and Industry; Information Technology Resource Center (computerized accounting project for nonprofit organizations)

Grants awarded to organizations located in the Chicago vicinity.

Typical grant range: $2,000 to $40,000

152

Harris Family Foundation
P.O. Box 2279
Northbrook, IL 60065
(708) 498-1261

Secondary education (computer department)

Most grants awarded to organizations located in Chicago.

Typical grant range: $1,000 to $10,000

153

Illinois Tool Works Foundation
3600 W. Lake Avenue
Glenview, IL 60025
(708) 724-7500

Teachers Academy for Mathematics and Science Teachers; General Motors Engineering and Management Institute

Grants awarded to organizations located in areas of company operations (Illinois Tool Works, Inc.), with an emphasis in Chicago.

Typical grant range: $1,000 to $15,000

154

Joyce Foundation
135 S. LaSalle Street, Suite 4010
Chicago, IL 60603
(312) 782-2464

Elementary schools (science education project); Chicago Public Schools (computer network for teachers)

Typical grant range: $5,000 to $75,000

155

John D. and Catherine T. MacArthur Foundation
140 S. Dearborn Street
Chicago, IL 60603
(312) 726-8000

Chicago Academy of Sciences; Museum of Science and Industry; Information Technology Resource Center (computer training for nonprofit organizations)

156

Nalco Foundation
One Nalco Center
Naperville, IL 60563
(708) 305-1556

Museum of Science and Industry; Science and Technology Interactive Center; Children's Hospital (laboratory information system)

Grants awarded to organizations located in areas of company operations (Nalco Chemical Co.).

Typical grant range: $1,000 to $12,000

157

Frank E. Payne and Seba B. Payne Foundation
c/o Bank of America
231 S. LaSalle Street
Chicago, IL 60697
(312) 828-1785

Hillside School (computer)

Typical grant range: $10,000 to $95,000

158

Polk Bros. Foundation, Inc.
420 N. Wabash Avenue, Suite 204
Chicago, IL 60611
(312) 527-4684

Minority students (mathematics tutoring program); Museum of Science and Industry; Better Boys Foundation (computer learning center)

Grants awarded to organizations located in the Chicago vicinity.

Typical grant range: $2,000 to $35,000

159
Rockford Community Trust
321 W. State Street, 13th Floor
Rockford, IL 61101
(815) 962-2110

Hunger Connection (computer); Tinker Swiss Cottage Museum (software); Children's Development Center (software); New American Theatre (high-tech sound equipment for people who are hearing impaired); Day Care Center (printer); Protestant Community Services (software); Rockford Area Affordable Housing Coalition (computer); Council on Aging (computer); YWCA (computer)

Grants awarded to organizations located in the Rockford vicinity.

Typical grant range: $500 to $8,000

160
Dr. Scholl Foundation
11 S. LaSalle Street, Suite 2100
Chicago, IL 60603
(312) 782-5210

Higher education (engineering, science); disabled (computer project); Museum of Science and Industry; Saint Thomas Aquinas High School (laptop computers)

Typical grant range: $5,000 to $40,000

INDIANA

161
Arvin Foundation, Inc.
One Noblitt Plaza
Box 3000
Columbus, IN 47202
(812) 379-3285

Higher education (engineering, science)

Grants awarded to organizations located in areas of company operations (Arvin Industries, Inc.).

Typical grant range: $100 to $4,000

162
Ball Brothers Foundation
222 S. Mulberry Street
P.O. Box 1408
Muncie, IN 47308
(317) 741-5500

Indiana Corporation for Science & Technology; Independent Colleges of Indiana Foundation (computer)

Grants awarded to organizations located in Indiana.

Typical grant range: $1,500 to $30,000

163
Clowes Fund, Inc.
250 E. 38th Street
Indianapolis, IN 46205
(317) 923-3264

Hospital (computer project); American Diabetes Association (computer project)

Typical grant range: $3,000 to $40,000

164
Community Foundation of Muncie and Delaware County, Inc.
P.O. Box 807
Muncie, IN 47308
(317) 747-7181

Computer grants; cultural organizations; community development

Grants awarded to organizations located in Delaware County and Muncie, Indiana.

Typical grant range: $2,000 to $12,000

165
Dekko Foundation, Inc.
P.O. Box 548
Kendallville, IN 46755
(219) 347-1278

Science Fair; Central Noble Community Schools (computer)

Typical grant range: $1,000 to $20,000

166
Elkhart County Community Foundation, Inc.
Ameritrust National Building
301 S. Main, P.O. Box 279
Elkhart, IN 46515
(219) 295-8761

Health organizations (fax machine); Big Brothers/Big Sisters (computer); American Red Cross (high-tech office equipment)

Grants awarded to organizations located in Elkhart County.

Typical grant range: $500 to $7,000

167
Heritage Fund of Bartholomew County, Inc.
430 Second Street
P.O. Box 1547
Columbus, IN 47202
(812) 376-7772

Arts Council (software)

Grants awarded to organizations located in Bartholomew County.

168
Indianapolis Foundation
615 N. Alabama Street, Room 119
Indianapolis, IN 46204
(317) 634-7497

Indianapolis Dance Company (computer); Indianapolis Public Schools (automate high school library); Community Centers of Indianapolis (computer training for low-income individuals); Children's Bureau of Indianapolis (computer, software); Meals on Wheels (computer training); Salvation Army (computer); United Way (computer project); YWCA (computer, software); Junior Achievement (computer); Indiana University Library (high-tech equipment)

Grants awarded to organizations located in the Indianapolis vicinity.

Typical grant range: $5,000 to $75,000

169
Irwin-Sweeney-Miller Foundation
420 Third Street
P.O. Box 808
Columbus, IN 47202
(812) 372-0251

Bartholomew Consolidated School Corporation (computer training for the alternative education program)

Grants awarded to organizations located in the Columbus vicinity.

Typical grant range: $750 to $10,000

170
Lilly Endowment Inc.
2801 N. Meridian Street
P.O. Box 88068
Indianapolis, IN 46208
(317) 924-5471

Secondary education (mathematics department); United Way (high-tech projects); Private Academic Library Network (computer, software)

Grants awarded to organizations located in Indiana, with an emphasis in Indianapolis.

Typical grant range: $2,500 to $60,000

171
M.E. Raker Foundation, Inc.
6207 Constitution Drive
Fort Wayne, IN 46804
(219) 436-2182

High school (computer laboratory); higher education (computer, copy machine); Washington House Treatment Center (computer)

Grants awarded to organizations located in Indiana, with an emphasis in Fort Wayne.

IOWA

172
Roy J. Carver Charitable Trust
P.O. Box 76
Muscatine, IA 52761
(319) 263-4010

Higher education (engineering, mathematics, science, scientific equipment)

Grants awarded to organizations located in Iowa.

Typical grant range: $25,000 to $200,000

173
Greater Cedar Rapids Foundation
101 Second Street, S.E., Suite 306
Cedar Rapids, IA 52401
(319) 366-2862

Boy Scouts (computer); Greater Cedar Rapids Foundation (software)

Grants awarded to organizations located in the Greater Cedar Rapids vicinity.

Typical grant range: $1,000 to $7,000

174
Hall Foundation, Inc.
115 Third Street, S.E., Suite 803
Cedar Rapids, IA 52401
(319) 362-9079

Higher education (computer network); Theater Cedar Rapids (computer)

Grants awarded to organizations located in the Cedar Rapids vicinity.

Typical grant range: $5,000 to $120,000

175
Hawley Foundation
1530 Financial Center
666 Walnut
Des Moines, IA 50309

Iowa School System (automate reference center); Lutheran Social Services (computer)

Grants awarded to organizations located in the Des Moines vicinity.

Typical grant range: $2,500 to $6,000

176
Kinney-Lindstrom Foundation, Inc.
P.O. Box 520
Mason City, IA 50401
(515) 896-3888

Public Library (computer project); North Iowa Fair (computer)

Grants awarded to organizations located in Iowa.

Typical grant range: $1,000 to $20,000

177
R.J. McElroy Trust
KWWL Building, Suite 318
500 E. Fourth Street
Waterloo, IA 50703
(319) 291-1299

Museum of History and Science (scientific equipment)

Typical grant range: $4,000 to $50,000

178
Pella Rolscreen Foundation
c/o Pella Corporation
102 Main Street
Pella, IA 50219
(515) 628-1000

Webster Elementary School (computer laboratory)

Grants awarded to organizations located in areas of company operations (Pella Corp.).

Typical grant range: $300 to $8,000

179
Van Buren Foundation, Inc.
c/o Farmers State Bank
Keosauqua, IA 52565
(319) 293-3794

Keosauqua Public Library (copy machine)

Grants awarded to organizations located in Van Buren County.

180

John H. Witte, Jr. Foundation
Firstar Bank Burlington, N.A.
P.O. Box 1088, 201 Jefferson Street
Burlington, IA 52601
(319) 752-2761

Higher education (scientific equipment);
Catholic Schools (computer); Planned
Parenthood (computer)

Grants awarded to organizations located
in the Burlington vicinity.

KANSAS

181

Bank IV Charitable Trust
c/o Bank IV Kansas, N.A.
P.O. Box 1122
Wichita, KS 67201
(316) 261-4361

Kansas State University Foundation
(College of Technology)

Grants awarded to organizations located
in areas of company operations (Bank IV
Kansas, N.A.).

Typical grant range: $1,000 to $15,000

182

Baughman Foundation
P.O. Box 1356
Liberal, KS 67905
(316) 624-1371

Ashland City Library (computer); City of
Kismet (software for the library); Meade
County Menonite Mission (software);
Shepherd of the Plains (computer)

Grants awarded to organizations located
in Kansas, with an emphasis in Liberal.

Typical grant range: $1,000 to $20,000

KENTUCKY

183

Margaret Hall Foundation, Inc.
291 S. Ashland Avenue
Lexington, KY 40502
(606) 269-2236

Secondary education (computer,
software); Research Academy for
Dyslexic Students (computer)

Typical grant range: $2,000 to $10,000

184

Herman H. Nettelroth Fund
c/o PNC Bank Kentucky
Citizens Plaza
Louisville, KY 40296
(502) 581-2399

Public Library (computer)

Grants awarded to organizations located
in Jefferson County.

Typical grant range: $4,000 to $15,000

LOUISIANA

185

Baton Rouge Area Foundation
One American Place, Suite 1740
Baton Rouge, LA 70825
(504) 387-6126

Health clinic (computer); Alcohol and
Drug Abuse Council (copy machine, fax
machine)

Grants awarded to organizations located
in the Baton Rouge vicinity.

186

**Edward G. Schlieder Educational
Foundation**
431 Gravier Street, Suite 400
New Orleans, LA 70130
(504) 581-6179

Secondary education (equipment for a
science laboratory)

Grants awarded to organizations located
in Louisiana.

Typical grant range: $15,000 to $50,000

MAINE

187
Simmons Foundation, Inc.
One Canal Plaza
Portland, ME 04101
(207) 774-2635

Governor Baxter's School for the Deaf
(computer); United Way (computer)

Grants awarded to organizations located
in Maine.

Typical grant range: $1,500 to $5,000

MARYLAND

188
Abell Foundation, Inc.
111 S. Calvert Street, Suite 2300
Baltimore, MD 21202
(410) 547-1300

Baltimore City Middle School Computer
Tournament; Druid Heights Community
Development Corporation (copy machine)

Grants awarded to organizations located
in Maryland, with an emphasis in
Baltimore.

Typical grant range: $3,000 to $50,000

189
Baltimore Community Foundation
The Latrobe Building
Two E. Read Street, 9th Floor
Baltimore, MD 21202
(410) 332-4171

Maryland Science Center; Maryland
Academy of Sciences; Baltimore Choral
Arts Society (software); After-School
Tutoring Program (computer)

Grants awarded to organizations located
in the Baltimore vicinity.

190
Emmert Hobbs Foundation, Inc.
c/o Friedman & Friedman
409 Washington Ave., Suite 900
Towson, MD 21204

Boys Latin School (computer center);
Learning Independence Thru Computers
(program for people with disabilities)

Grants awarded to organizations located
in the Baltimore vicinity.

Typical grant range: $2,000 to $10,000

191
**Marion I. and Henry J. Knott
Foundation, Inc.**
3904 Hickory Avenue
Baltimore, MD 21211
(410) 235-7068

Maryland Lupus Foundation (upgrade
computer); Queen of Peace School
(software); Changing Directions
(computer)

Typical grant range: $1,000 to $25,000

192
Middendorf Foundation, Inc.
Five E. Read Street
Baltimore, MD 21202
(410) 752-7088

Boys Latin School Science Department
(computer, scientific equipment)

Grants awarded to organizations located
in Maryland.

Typical grant range: $1,000 to $25,000

MASSACHUSETTS

193
Boston Foundation, Inc.
One Boston Place, 24th Floor
Boston, MA 02108
(617) 723-7415

Middle schools (algebra project); youth
organizations (computer training);
Information Center for Individuals with
Disabilities (computer project)

Grants awarded to organizations located
in the Boston vicinity.

Typical grant range: $10,000 to $55,000

194
Cabot Corporation Foundation, Inc.
75 State Street
Boston, MA 02109
(617) 345-0100

Higher education (science, engineering,
computer science); Museum of Science
(science laboratory)

Grants awarded to organizations located
in areas of company operations (Cabot
Corp.).

195
**Community Foundation of Western
Massachusetts**
1500 Main Street, Suite 1800
P.O. Box 15769
Springfield, MA 01115
(413) 732-2858

The School, Inc. (computer laboratory);
Abortion Rights Fund (computer)

Grants awarded to organizations located
in western Massachusetts.

196
**Ruth H. and Warren A. Ellsworth
Foundation**
370 Main Street, 12th Floor
Worcester, MA 01608
(508) 798-8621

Higher education (science, engineering);
Worcester Foundation for Experimental
Biology; New England Science Center

Grants awarded to organizations located
in the Worcester vicinity.

Typical grant range: $2,000 to $25,000

197
Island Foundation, Inc.
589 Mill Street
Marion, MA 02738
(508) 748-2809

Save-the-Bay (wastewater treatment
technology project); Latino Access Center
(software, printer)

Typical grant range: $2,000 to $15,000

198
Ellis L. Phillips Foundation
29 Commonwealth Avenue
Boston, MA 02116
(617) 424-7607

Higher education (computer training);
Computer Museum; School of Music
(computer for the library)

Typical grant range: $2,000 to $10,000

199
Polaroid Foundation, Inc.
750 Main Street, 2M
Cambridge, MA 02139
(617) 386-8351

Computer Museum; Massachusetts Pre-
Engineering Program; Rowland Institute
of Science

Grants awarded to organizations located
in Massachusetts.

Typical grant range: $1,000 to $12,000

200
State Street Foundation
c/o State Street Bank and Trust Co.
P.O. Box 351
Boston, MA 02101
(617) 654-3381

Computer Museum; Massachusetts Institute of Technology (scientific research)

Grants awarded to organizations located in the Boston vicinity.

Typical grant range: $5,000 to $75,000

MICHIGAN

201
Battle Creek Community Foundation
One Riverwalk Center
34 W. Jackson Street
Battle Creek, MI 49017
(616) 962-2181

Battle Creek Area Mathematics and Science Center; RESOLVE (computer project for mediation organization); Haven of Rest Mission (computer, printer); Kingman Museum (science project); Council of Michigan Foundations (computer project); Albion College (science program for minorities)

Grants awarded to organizations located in the Battle Creek vicinity.

Typical grant range: $1,000 to $20,000

202
Bauervic-Paisley Foundation
2855 Coolidge Highway, Suite 100
Troy, MI 48084

Kensington Academy (computer project)

Typical grant range: $1,000 to $15,000

203
Besser Foundation
123 N. Second Avenue, Suite 4
Alpena, MI 49707
(517) 354-4722

Alpena Public Schools (computer laboratory); Legal Services of Northern Michigan (computer)

Most grants awarded to organizations located in Alpena.

Typical grant range: $4,000 to $50,000

204
A.G. Bishop Charitable Trust
c/o NBD Bank, N.A.
One E. First Street
Flint, MI 48502
(810) 760-8451

Outreach Ministries (computer); Planned Parenthood (computer); Executive Service Association (copy machine)

Grants awarded to organizations located in the Flint vicinity.

205
Community Foundation for Northeast Michigan
123 Water Street
P.O. Box 282
Alpena, MI 49707
(517) 354-6881

St. Mary's School (computer); Depressive and Manic-Depressive Association (copy machine); Alcona County Committee on Aging (copy machine); Child and Family Services (computer)

Grants awarded to organizations located in the Alpena County vicinity.

Typical grant range: $400 to $5,000

206
Community Foundation for Southeastern Michigan
333 W. Fort Street, Suite 2010
Detroit, MI 48226
(313) 961-6675

Higher education (mathematics department); Deaf, Hearing and Speech Center (assistive technology program); Council of Michigan Foundations (computer project)

Grants awarded to organizations located in southeastern Michigan.

Typical grant range: $1,000 to $25,000

207
Ford Motor Company Fund
The American Road
Dearborn, MI 48121
(313) 845-8711

Higher education (engineering, science); Henry Ford Community College (engineering)

Grants awarded to organizations located in areas of company operations (Ford Motor Company), with an emphasis in Detroit.

Typical grant range: $1,500 to $30,000

208
Frey Foundation
48 Fountain Street, N.W., Suite 200
Grand Rapids, MI 49503
(616) 451-0303

Michigan Housing Coalition (copy machine); Saint Andrew's School (computer, software, computer training)

Typical grant range: $10,000 to $30,000

209
General Motors Foundation, Inc.
13-145 General Motors Building
3044 W. Grand Blvd.
Detroit, MI 48202
(313) 556-4260

Higher education (engineering); Minorities in Science and Engineering; Detroit Science Center

Grants awarded to organizations located in areas of company operations (General Motors Corp.).

Typical grant range: $2,000 to $125,000

210
Grand Haven Area Community Foundation, Inc.
One South Harbor
Grand Haven, MI 49417
(616) 842-6378

Elderly (computer, software); Public Library (computer); Nature Center (copy machine)

Grants awarded to organizations located in the Grand Haven vicinity.

Typical grant range: $1,000 to $12,000

211
Herrick Foundation
150 W. Jefferson, Suite 2500
Detroit, MI 48226
(313) 496-7656

Association for Retarded Citizens (computer)

Most grants awarded to organizations located in Michigan.

Typical grant range: $5,000 to $75,000

212
Jackson Community Foundation
230 W. Michigan Avenue
Jackson, MI 49201
(517) 787-1321

Cultural organizations (computer)

Grants awarded to organizations located in Jackson County.

Typical grant range: $1,500 to $25,000

213
Kalamazoo Foundation
151 S. Rose Street, Suite 332
Kalamazoo, MI 49007
(616) 381-4416

Kalamazoo Area Math and Science
Center; Legal Aid Bureau (computer
project); Kalamazoo Valley Intermediate
School District (high-tech interactive
classroom project for high schools)

Grants awarded to organizations located
in Kalamazoo County.

214
Louis G. Kaufman Endowment Fund
MFC First National Bank
P.O. Box 580
Marquette, MI 49855
(906) 228-1244

Marquette Area Public Schools
(computer); Father Marquette Catholic
School (computer laboratory)

Grants awarded to organizations located
in Marquette.

Typical grant range: $1,000 to $9,000

215
W.K. Kellogg Foundation
One Michigan Avenue East
Battle Creek, MI 49017
(616) 968-1611

Secondary education (technology
education program); higher education
(engineering, science); Challenger Center
for Space Science Education

216
Kresge Foundation
P.O. Box 3151
3215 W. Big Beaver Road
Troy, MI 48007
(810) 643-9630

Public Library (high-tech equipment);
Hope College, Division of Natural
Sciences and Mathematics (laboratory
equipment); United Community Services
of Metropolitan Detroit (computer);
Luther College (scientific equipment)

Typical grant range: $125,000 to $600,000

217
Frances Goll Mills Fund
Second National Bank of Saginaw
101 N. Washington Avenue
Saginaw, MI 48607
(517) 776-7405

American Red Cross (computer); City
Rescue Mission (software); Zavel
Memorial Library (computer)

Grants awarded to organizations located
in Saginaw County.

Typical grant range: $1,000 to $9,000

218
Steelcase Foundation
Location CH.5C
P.O. Box 1967
Grand Rapids, MI 49501
(616) 246-4695

Saint Andrew's School (mathematics,
science); Aquinas College (Mathematics
Computer Laboratory)

Grants awarded to organizations located
in areas of company operations (Steelcase,
Inc.).

Typical grant range: $2,000 to $30,000

219
Upjohn Company Foundation
7000 Portage Road
Kalamazoo, MI 49001
(616) 323-7017

National Action Council for Minorities in
Engineering; Kalamazoo Area Math and
Science Center

Most grants awarded to organizations
located in the Kalamazoo vicinity.

220
Harvey Randall Wickes Foundation
Plaza North, Suite 472
4800 Fashion Square Blvd.
Saginaw, MI 48604
(517) 799-1850

Voluntary Action Center (computer)

Grants awarded to organizations located
in the Saginaw vicinity.

Typical grant range: $5,000 to $40,000

221
Matilda R. Wilson Fund
100 Renaissance Center, 33rd Floor
Detroit, MI 48243
(313) 259-7777

Detroit Science Center; Mathematical
Association of America

Typical grant range: $15,000 to $50,000

MINNESOTA

222
F.R. Bigelow Foundation
600 Norwest Center
St. Paul, MN 55101
(612) 224-5463

United Way (computer); College of Saint
Benedict (building funds for the Science
Center)

Grants awarded to organizations located
in the St. Paul vicinity.

Typical grant range: $5,000 to $50,000

223
Blandin Foundation
100 Pokegama Avenue North
Grand Rapids, MN 55744
(218) 326-0523

Arrowhead Community College
Foundation (science laboratory);
University of Minnesota (technology
transfer program)

Grants awarded to organizations located
in Minnesota.

Typical grant range: $5,000 to $75,000

224
Otto Bremer Foundation
445 Minnesota Street, Suite 2000
St. Paul, MN 55101
(612) 227-8036

Higher education (computer project for a
library); Head Start (computer)

Grants awarded to organizations located
in areas of company operations (Bremer
Bank).

Typical grant range: $2,000 to $20,000

225
Bush Foundation
E-900 First National Bank Bldg.
332 Minnesota Street
St. Paul, MN 55101
(612) 227-0891

American Indian Science and Engineering
Society; higher education (mathematics,
science, engineering)

Typical grant range: $30,000 to $100,000

226
Cray Research Foundation
655A Loan Oak Drive
Eagan, MN 55121
(612) 683-7379

Higher education (mathematics,
engineering, computer science)

Most grants awarded to organizations
located in Minnesota.

Typical grant range: $1,500 to $25,000

227
General Mills Foundation
P.O. Box 1113
Minneapolis, MN 55440
(612) 540-7891

Science Museum of Minnesota; Center for Independence, Training and Education (computer project for children who are visually impaired)

Grants awarded to organizations located in areas of company operations (General Mills, Inc.).

Typical grant range: $3,000 to $25,000

228
Honeywell Foundation
Honeywell Plaza
P.O. Box 524
Minneapolis, MN 55440
(612) 951-2231

American Indian Science and Engineering Society; Museum of Science and Technology; Minnesota High Technology Foundation

Grants awarded to organizations located in areas of company operations (Honeywell, Inc.), with an emphasis in Minneapolis.

Typical grant range: $1,000 to $25,000

229
Emma B. Howe Memorial Foundation
A200 Foshay Tower
821 Marquette Avenue
Minneapolis, MN 55402
(612) 339-7343

People Achieving Change Through Technology (high-tech project for people with disabilities)

Grants awarded to organizations located in Minnesota.

Typical grant range: $5,000 to $30,000

230
Mardag Foundation
600 Norwest Center
St. Paul, MN 55101
(612) 224-5463

Minnesota Council on Foundations (computer project); South Central Minnesota Inner City Library (software)

Grants awarded to organizations located in Minnesota.

Typical grant range: $5,000 to $50,000

231
McKnight Foundation
Suite 600 TCF Tower
121 S. Eighth Street
Minneapolis, MN 55402
(612) 333-4220

Family and Children's Service (computer); Saint David's School for Child Development and Family Services (computer)

Grants awarded to organizations located in Minnesota.

Typical grant range: $20,000 to $200,000

232
Medtronic Foundation
7000 Central Avenue, N.E.
Minneapolis, MN 55432
(612) 574-3024

Higher education (science department); National Action Council for Minorities in Engineering; Museum of Science and Technology

Grants awarded to organizations located in areas of company operations (Medtronic, Inc.).

Typical grant range: $3,000 to $15,000

233

Minneapolis Foundation
A200 Foshay Tower
821 Marquette Avenue, South
Minneapolis, MN 55402
(612) 339-7343

Fremont Community Health Services
(software)

Grants awarded to organizations located
in Minnesota, with an emphasis in the
Minneapolis-St. Paul vicinity.

Typical grant range: $1,000 to $25,000

234

**Minnesota Mining and Manufacturing
Foundation, Inc.**
3M Center Building 591-30-02
St. Paul, MN 55144

Higher education (engineering, science,
computer science, minorities); Science
Museum of Minnesota

Grants awarded to organizations located
in areas of company operations
(Minnesota Mining and Manufacturing
Co.).

Typical grant range: $500 to $20,000

235

Ordean Foundation
501 Ordean Building
424 W. Superior Street
Duluth, MN 55802
(218) 726-4785

Operation Aware (copy machine); Spectra
(computer, software)

Typical grant range: $500 to $25,000

236

Rochester Area Foundation
1815 14th Street, N.W.
Rochester, MN 55901
(507) 282-0203

Family Service Rochester, Inc. (software)

Grants awarded to organizations located
in Olmsted County.

Typical grant range: $1,000 to $11,000

237

Saint Paul Foundation, Inc.
600 Norwest Center
St. Paul, MN 55101
(612) 224-5463

Management Assistance Project for
Nonprofits, Inc. (computer)

Grants awarded to organizations located
in the St. Paul vicinity.

Typical grant range: $1,000 to $30,000

MISSOURI

238

Guy I. Bromley Residuary Trust
c/o Boatmen's First National Bank of
Kansas City
14 W. 10th Street
Kansas City, MO 64183
(816) 691-7481

Cooperative Social Services (computer)

239

Community Foundation of the Ozarks
901 St. Louis Street, Suite 303
Springfield, MO 65806
(417) 864-6199

Science Museum; dyslexia (computer
project); KSMU (microwave transmission
system)

Most grants awarded to organizations
located in Greene County.

240

Louetta M. Cowden Foundation
Boatmen's First National Bank of
Kansas City
P.O. Box 419038
Kansas City, MO 64105

Domestic Violence Network (software);
Literacy Council (computer)

Few grants awarded.

Grants awarded to organizations located
in the Kansas City vicinity.

Typical grant range: $10,000 to $40,000

241
Greater Kansas City Community Foundation and Affiliated Trusts
1055 Broadway, Suite 130
Kansas City, MO 64105
(816) 842-0944

Kansas City Public Library (automation project); United Way (computer project)

Grants awarded to organizations located in the Kansas City vicinity.

Typical grant range: $5,000 to $25,000

242
McDonnell Douglas Foundation
P.O. Box 516, Mail Code 1001510
St. Louis, MO 63166
(314) 234-0360

Higher education (engineering, science, mathematics); St. Louis Science Center

Grants awarded to organizations located in areas of company operations (McDonnell Douglas Corp.).

Typical grant range: $5,000 to $12,000

243
James S. McDonnell Foundation
1034 S. Brentwood Blvd., Suite 1610
St. Louis, MO 63117
(314) 721-1532

Higher education (science, mathematics); St. Louis Science Center

Typical grant range: $50,000 to $250,000

244
St. Louis Community Foundation
818 Olive Street, Suite 935
St. Louis, MO 63101
(314) 241-2703

Computer projects; disabled; community development; scientific research; engineering; Science Center

Grants awarded to organizations located in the St. Louis vicinity.

Typical grant range: $500 to $9,000

245
Courtney S. Turner Charitable Trust
c/o Boatmen's First National Bank of Kansas City
P.O. Box 419038
Kansas City, MO 64183
(816) 691-7481

Westminster College (computer); University of Missouri (word processors); Girl Scouts (computer project)

Typical grant range: $3,000 to $80,000

246
Union Electric Company Charitable Trust
1901 Chouteau Street
P.O. Box 149, Mail Code 100
St. Louis, MO 63166
(314) 554-2902

Higher education (engineering); St. Louis Science Center

Grants awarded to organizations located in areas of company operations (Union Electric Company).

Typical grant range: $5,000 to $35,000

MONTANA

247
Montana Community Foundation
Power Block Building, Suite 4-1
Seven W. Sixth Avenue
Helena, MT 59601
(406) 443-8313

Mental Health Foundation (computer, printer); Butte Family YMCA (computer training, printer)

Grants awarded to organizations located in Montana.

NEBRASKA

248
Fremont Area Community Foundation
92 W. Fifth Street
P.O. Box 182
Fremont, NE 68025
(402) 721-4252

North Bend Library Foundation
(computer)

Grants awarded to organizations located
in the Fremont vicinity.

249
Hamilton Community Foundation, Inc.
1108 L Street
P.O. Box 283
Aurora, NE 68818
(402) 694-3200

New Miami School District (computer
write to read program)

Grants awarded to organizations located
in Hamilton County.

Typical grant range: $500 to $2,000

250
Kaufmann-Cummings Trust
c/o FirsTier Bank, N.A.
P.O. Box 2006
Grand Island, NE 68802

Bellevue College (computer for the
library)

Grants awarded to organizations located
in Nebraska.

Typical grant range: $500 to $20,000

251
Peter Kiewit Foundation
900 Woodmen Tower
17th and Farnam Streets
Omaha, NE 68102
(402) 344-7890

Higher education (automate library)

252
Lincoln Foundation, Inc.
215 Centennial Mall South, Suite 200
Lincoln, NE 68508
(402) 474-2345

Lancaster County Medical Society
(computer project); Planned Parenthood
(computer); Malone Community Center
Foundation (computer)

Most grants awarded to organizations
located in the Lincoln vicinity.

Typical grant range: $1,000 to $6,000

253
**Mid-Nebraska Community
Foundation, Inc.**
410 Rodeo Road
P.O. Box 1321
North Platte, NE 69103
(308) 534-3315

North Platte Opportunity Center
(computer)

254
Pamida Foundation
P.O. Box 3856
Omaha, NE 68103
(402) 339-2400

City of New Hampton Public Library
(microfilm equipment)

Grants awarded to organizations located
in areas of company operations (Pamida,
Inc.).

Typical grant range: $300 to $1,500

255
Robert D. Wilson Foundation
Guarantee Center, Suite 280
8805 Indian Hills Drive
Omaha, NE 68114
(402) 390-0390

Computer grants; social welfare; youth
organizations; alcohol abuse

Grants awarded to organizations located
in Nebraska.

Typical grant range: $2,500 to $8,000

NEVADA

256
Cord Foundation
200 Court Street
Reno, NV 89501
(702) 323-0373

Disabled (computer); secondary education (computer training); Washoe County Law Library (computer project)

Most grants awarded to organizations located in northern Nevada.

Typical grant range: $5,000 to $50,000

257
E.L. Wiegand Foundation
Wiegand Center
165 W. Liberty Street
Reno, NV 89501
(702) 333-0310

Higher education (science laboratory); performing arts (computer); Good Shepherd School (computer); Jesuit High School (science equipment)

Most grants awarded to Roman Catholic organizations.

Typical grant range: $5,000 to $75,000

NEW HAMPSHIRE

258
Agnes M. Lindsay Trust
238 Central Street
Hudson, NH 03051
(603) 598-0655

Hospice (computer); Mid Coast Health Services (computer); Community Service Project (copy machine); Mohawk Valley Health Education Services (computer)

Typical grant range: $1,500 to $7,500

259
New Hampshire Charitable Foundation
37 Pleasant Street
Concord, NH 03301
(603) 225-6641

Tin Mountain Conservation Center (computer)

Grants awarded to organizations located in New Hampshire.

Typical grant range: $2,000 to $8,000

260
Walker Foundation
P.O. Box 614
Hollis, NH 03049

School District (computer, software, electronic encyclopedia); School Administrative Unit (science data collection equipment)

Grants awarded to organizations located in New Hampshire.

Typical grant range: $1,000 to $12,000

NEW JERSEY

261
AlliedSignal Foundation
P.O. Box 2245
Morristown, NJ 07962
(201) 455-5877

Higher education (engineering, science, mathematics); Fairleigh Dickinson University (science department)

Grants awarded to organizations located in areas of company operations (AlliedSignal, Inc.).

Typical grant range: $1,000 to $12,000

262
Emil Buehler Perpetual Trust
305 Route 17
Paramus, NJ 07652
(201) 262-6292

Buehler Challenger and Science Center; Museum of Discovery and Science

Typical grant range: $500 to $10,000

263

Geraldine R. Dodge Foundation, Inc.
163 Madison Avenue
P.O. Box 1239
Morristown, NJ 07962
(201) 540-8442

Secondary education (mathematics, science, minorities); Liberty Science Center and Hall of Technology

Typical grant range: $5,000 to $45,000

264

Charles Edison Fund
101 S. Harrison Street
East Orange, NJ 07018
(201) 675-9000

Higher education (engineering, science)

Typical grant range: $500 to $10,000

265

Fund for the New Jersey Blind, Inc.
153 Halsey Street
P.O. Box 47017
Newark, NJ 07101
(201) 648-2324

National Federation of the Blind (computer); RP Foundation of Princeton (high-tech equipment for retinal research)

Grants awarded to organizations located in New Jersey.

Typical grant range: $500 to $5,000

266

Hyde and Watson Foundation
437 Southern Blvd.
Chatham, NJ 07928
(201) 966-6024

Computer grants; software grants; child welfare; health organizations; performing arts; community development; American Red Cross (computer); Chemocare (computer)

Typical grant range: $5,000 to $25,000

267

F.M. Kirby Foundation, Inc.
17 DeHart Street
P.O. Box 151
Morristown, NJ 07963
(201) 538-4800

Coriell Institute for Medical Research (computer); Girl Scouts (computer)

Typical grant range: $10,000 to $25,000

268

Blanche and Irving Laurie Foundation, Inc.
P.O. Box 53
Roseland, NJ 07068
(201) 535-5557

Hospital (computer); Learning Computer Resource Institute

Grants awarded to organizations located in New Jersey.

Typical grant range: $500 to $30,000

269

Merck Company Foundation
One Merck Drive
P.O. Box 100
Whitehouse Station, NJ 08889
(908) 423-2042

Higher education (science, engineering); scientific equipment; Merck Institute for Science Education

Grants awarded to organizations located in areas of company operations (Merck & Co., Inc.).

Typical grant range: $5,000 to $45,000

270

Fannie E. Rippel Foundation
180 Mount Airy Road, Suite 200
Basking Ridge, NJ 07920

Children's Hospital (computer); Rider College (scientific equipment for biology department)

Typical grant range: $75,000 to $200,000

271
Turrell Fund
21 Van Vleck Street
Montclair, NJ 07042
(201) 783-9358

Upsala College (science program); Girl
Scouts (science program)

Most grants awarded to organizations
located in New Jersey.

Typical grant range: $5,000 to $35,000

272
**Warner-Lambert Charitable
Foundation**
201 Tabor Road
Morris Plains, NJ 07950
(201) 540-3652

Liberty Science Center and Hall of
Technology

Grants awarded to organizations located
in areas of company operations (Warner-
Lambert Co.).

Typical grant range: $5,000 to $30,000

273
Westfield Foundation
301 North Avenue West
P.O. Box 2295
Westfield, NJ 07091
(908) 233-9787

Community development (copy machine)

Grants awarded to organizations located
in Westfield.

NEW MEXICO

274
**Marshall & Perrine D. McCune
Charitable Foundation**
123 E. Marcy Street, Suite 201
Santa Fe, NM 87501
(505) 983-8300

Jobs for Progress (computer laboratory)

Grants awarded to organizations located
in New Mexico.

Typical grant range: $3,000 to $40,000

NEW YORK

275
Altman Foundation
220 E. 42nd Street, Suite 411
New York, NY 10017
(212) 682-0970

Middle school (mathematics, science);
higher education (mathematics, science
programs for minorities)

Grants awarded to organizations located
in New York City.

Typical grant range: $5,000 to $100,000

276
The Area Fund
Nine Vassar Street
Poughkeepsie, NY 12601
(914) 452-3077

High-tech equipment; cultural
organizations; environment

Grants awarded to organizations located
in Dutchess County.

Typical grant range: $300 to $4,000

277
AT&T Foundation
1301 Avenue of the Americas, Suite 3100
New York, NY 10019
(212) 841-4747

Higher education (electrical engineering,
mathematics, science, computer science)

Typical grant range: $5,000 to $40,000

278
**Rose M. Badgeley Residuary
Charitable Trust**
c/o Marine Midland Bank, N.A.
250 Park Avenue
New York, NY 10177
(212) 503-2786

Make-A-Wish Foundation (computer)

Typical grant range: $5,000 to $20,000

279
Bodman Foundation
767 Third Avenue, 4th Floor
New York, NY 10017
(212) 644-0322

Public schools (computer education
project); Columbia University-Teachers
College (building funds for a science
laboratory)

Grants awarded to organizations located
in the New York City vicinity.

Typical grant range: $15,000 to $50,000

280
Booth Ferris Foundation
c/o Morgan Guaranty Trust Co. of
New York
60 Wall Street, 46th Floor
New York, NY 10260
(212) 809-1630

Higher education (science department);
New York Hall of Science

Grants awarded to organizations located
in the New York City vicinity.

Typical grant range: $20,000 to $100,000

281
Buffalo Foundation
1601 Main-Seneca Building
237 Main Street
Buffalo, NY 14203
(716) 852-2857

Public Library (microfilming project);
Cradle Beach Camp (computer); Legal
Aid Bureau (computer); Life Transitions
Center (computer); Clarence Center
Elementary School (computer, software);
Effective Parenting Information for
Children (computer); Jewish Community
Center (computer); Buffalo Seminary
(computer training)

Grants awarded to organizations located
in Erie County.

Typical grant range: $1,000 to $14,000

282
Louis Calder Foundation
230 Park Avenue, Room 1525
New York, NY 10169
(212) 687-1680

Brooklyn Bureau of Community Service
(computer project for the child care
center); New York Hall of Science
(educational program); Goodwill
Industries (computer training)

Most grants awarded to organizations
located in New York City.

Typical grant range: $10,000 to $40,000

283
Carnegie Corporation of New York
437 Madison Avenue
New York, NY 10022
(212) 371-3200

National Action Council for Minorities in
Engineering; American Association for
the Advancement of Science; Rockefeller
University (science education)

Grants awarded to organizations located
throughout the United States.

284
**Central New York Community
Foundation, Inc.**
500 S. Salina Street, Suite 428
Syracuse, NY 13202
(315) 422-9538

Legal Aid Society (computer project);
Museum of Science and Technology
(high-tech office equipment); Mental
Health Association (computer training);
Onondaga County Public Library (Internet
Training Center)

Grants awarded to organizations located
in Onondaga and Madison Counties.

285
Chautauqua Region Community Foundation, Inc.
104-106 Hotel Jamestown Building
Jamestown, NY 14701
(716) 661-3390

American Heart Association (computer); American Red Cross (computer); Legal Services for the Elderly (computer)

Grants awarded to organizations located in Chautauqua County.

Typical grant range: $1,000 to $9,000

286
Clark Foundation
30 Wall Street
New York, NY 10005
(212) 269-1833

Waterford Institute (computer training); Research Foundation of the State University of New York (computer)

Typical grant range: $15,000 to $80,000

287
Robert Sterling Clark Foundation, Inc.
112 East 64th Street
New York, NY 10021
(212) 308-0411

Museum (computer); Volunteer Lawyers for the Arts (computer); Downtown Music Productions (computer)

Most grants awarded to organizations located in the New York City vicinity.

Typical grant range: $10,000 to $75,000

288
Community Foundation for the Capital Region, N.Y.
P.O. Box 3198
Albany, NY 12203
(518) 273-8596

Abused women (computer); literacy (computer training)

Grants awarded to organizations located in Albany, Rensselaer, and Saratoga Counties.

Typical grant range: $500 to $2,500

289
Corning Incorporated Foundation
MP-LB-02-1
Corning, NY 14831
(607) 974-8746

Higher education (science, engineering); Boy Scouts (computer); Cornell University (engineering)

Grants awarded to organizations located in areas of company operations (Corning Inc.).

Typical grant range: $500 to $2,000

290
James H. Cummings Foundation, Inc.
1807 Elmwood Avenue, Suite 112
Buffalo, NY 14207
(716) 874-0040

Meals on Wheels (copy machine); Longview Niagara (computer)

Typical grant range: $2,000 to $50,000

291
Aaron Diamond Foundation, Inc.
1270 Avenue of the Americas, Suite 2624
New York, NY 10020
(212) 757-7680

Science Skills Center; National Action Council for Minorities in Engineering; New York Youth Network (computer bulletin board); Columbia University-Teachers College (Technology Education Program)

Grants awarded to organizations located in New York City.

Typical grant range: $15,000 to $60,000

292
Camille and Henry Dreyfus Foundation, Inc.
555 Madison Avenue, Suite 1305
New York, NY 10022
(212) 753-1760

Higher education (chemistry); Museum of Science and Industry; New York Academy of Sciences

Typical grant range: $5,000 to $40,000

293
Eastman Kodak Charitable Trust
c/o Eastman Kodak Company
343 State Street
Rochester, NY 14650
(716) 724-2434

Middle school (mathematics laboratory);
Rochester City School District (science
department); Rochester Engineering Entry
Program (computer, software)

Grants awarded to organizations located
in areas of company operations (Eastman
Kodak Co.).

Typical grant range: $3,000 to $40,000

294
Helene Fuld Health Trust
c/o Townley & Updike
405 Lexington Avenue
New York, NY 10174
(212) 973-6859

Higher education (computer assisted
instruction and high-tech equipment for
nursing schools); hospital (computer
assisted instruction for training nurses)

Typical grant range: $10,000 to $50,000

295
Gebbie Foundation, Inc.
Hotel Jamestown Building, Suite 308
P.O. Box 1277
Jamestown, NY 14702
(716) 487-1062

Southwestern Independent Living Center
(copy machine); Fenton Historical Society
(computer)

Most grants awarded to organizations
located in Chautauqua County.

Typical grant range: $2,000 to $35,000

296
Herman Goldman Foundation
61 Broadway, 18th Floor
New York, NY 10006
(212) 797-9090

Higher education (computer science,
mathematics); Science Museum; Long
Island Jewish Medical Center (computer)

Grants awarded to organizations located
in the New York City vicinity.

Typical grant range: $5,000 to $40,000

297
Greenwall Foundation
Two Park Avenue, 24th Floor
New York, NY 10016
(212) 679-7266

National Action Council for Minorities in
Engineering; City College of the City
University of New York (workshop for
middle school mathematics teachers);
New York Hall of Science (workshop for
elementary and middle school teachers)

Most grants awarded to organizations
located in the New York City vicinity.

Typical grant range: $4,000 to $35,000

298
John A. Hartford Foundation, Inc.
55 E. 59th Street
New York, NY 10022
(212) 832-7788

Hospital (computer project); health
organization (computer project)

Typical grant range: $35,000 to $350,000

299
Charles Hayden Foundation
One Bankers Trust Plaza
130 Liberty Street
New York, NY 10006
(212) 938-0790

Family Math at City Tech; New York Hall
of Science; Aquinas High School
(building funds for a biology laboratory)

Typical grant range: $15,000 to $125,000

300

William Randolph Hearst Foundation
888 Seventh Avenue
New York, NY 10106
(212) 586-5404

Elementary school (computer); Museum
of Science and Industry

Typical grant range: $15,000 to $70,000

301

F.B. Heron Foundation
c/o Rockefeller Financial Services, Inc.
30 Rockefeller Plaza, Rm. 5600
New York, NY 10112
(212) 649-5612

United Neighborhood Houses of New
York (computer project)

Typical grant range: $15,000 to $50,000

302

Hugoton Foundation
900 Park Avenue
New York, NY 10021

High school (science equipment); USO of
Metro New York (computer); Pace
University-School of Nursing (computer)

Typical grant range: $5,000 to $35,000

303

Roger Kresge Foundation, Inc.
320 N. McKinley Avenue
Endicott, NY 13760
(607) 748-4040

Kopernik Observatory (Science Center)

Grants awarded to organizations located
in Broome County.

304

Henry Luce Foundation, Inc.
111 W. 50th Street, Suite 3710
New York, NY 10020
(212) 489-7700

Higher education (science and
engineering programs for women)

Typical grant range: $15,000 to $175,000

305

Andrew W. Mellon Foundation
140 E. 62nd Street
New York, NY 10021
(212) 838-8400

Higher education (establish digital
library); Institute of Electrical and
Electronic Engineers

306

**Merrill Lynch & Company
Foundation, Inc.**
South Tower, 6th Floor
World Financial Center
New York, NY 10080
(212) 236-4319

Liberty Science Center and Hall of
Technology; New York Academy of
Sciences; Canisius College (science
department)

Grants awarded to organizations located
in areas of company operations (Merrill
Lynch & Company, Inc.), with an
emphasis in the New York City vicinity.

Typical grant range: $3,000 to $40,000

307

Metropolitan Life Foundation
One Madison Avenue
New York, NY 10010
(212) 578-6272

Museum of Science and Industry; Science
and Technology Interactive Center

Typical grant range: $1,500 to $30,000

308

NEC Foundation of America
Eight Old Sod Farm Road
Melville, NY 11747
(516) 753-7021

Higher education (science, engineering,
computer science); Foundation for
Technology Access; Center for Computer
Assistance to the Disabled; Junior
Engineering Technical Society

Typical grant range: $5,000 to $30,000

309
New York Community Trust
Two Park Avenue, 24th Floor
New York, NY 10016
(212) 686-0010

Science Skills Center (mathematics and science program); Saint Mary's Hospital for Children (computer); YWCA (computer training)

Grants awarded to organizations located in the New York City vicinity.

Typical grant range: $5,000 to $45,000

310
NYNEX Foundation
1095 Avenue of the Americas
New York, NY 10036

Science Center (software); Recording for the Blind (high-tech equipment)

Grants awarded to organizations located in areas of company operations (NYNEX Corp.).

Typical grant range: $15,000 to $75,000

311
A. Lindsay and Olive B. O'Connor Foundation
P.O. Box D
Hobart, NY 13788
(607) 538-9248

Girl Scouts (copy machine); Roxbury Arts Group (computer, software)

Typical grant range: $2,000 to $30,000

312
F.W. Olin Foundation, Inc.
780 Third Avenue
New York, NY 10017
(212) 832-0508

Higher education (building funds for the science and computer science departments)

Few grants awarded.

313
Pinkerton Foundation
725 Park Avenue
New York, NY 10021
(212) 772-6110

Center for Applied Special Technology

Grants awarded to organizations located in New York City.

Typical grant range: $10,000 to $30,000

314
Charles H. Revson Foundation, Inc.
444 Madison Avenue, 30th Floor
New York, NY 10022
(212) 935-3340

Waterford Institute (computer project for New York City Schools)

Typical grant range: $5,000 to $100,000

315
Dorothea Haus Ross Foundation
1036 Monroe Avenue
Rochester, NY 14620
(716) 473-6006

Cerebral Palsy Treatment Center (computer project)

Typical grant range: $1,000 to $8,000

316
Ralph C. Sheldon Foundation, Inc.
P.O. Box 417
Jamestown, NY 14702
(716) 664-9890

Public Library (computer); YMCA (computer); Chautauqua Adult Day Care (copy machine)

Most grants awarded to organizations located in Chautauqua County.

Typical grant range: $10,000 to $65,000

317
Sony USA Foundation, Inc.
Nine W. 57th Street
New York, NY 10019
(212) 418-9404

National Action Council for Minorities in Engineering; Challenger Center for Space Science Education

Typical grant range: $500 to $50,000

318
Toshiba America Foundation
1251 Ave. of the Americas
New York, NY 10020
(212) 596-0600

AMN High School (mathematics);
Clearwater Central Catholic High School
(computer project); Colby High School
(high-tech equipment)

Grants awarded to organizations located
in areas of company operations (Toshiba
America, Inc.).

Typical grant range: $1,000 to $20,000

319
Utica Foundation, Inc.
270 Genesee Street
Utica, NY 13502
(315) 735-8212

Holland Free Library (computer,
software); Central New York Arts Council
(computer); Utica Symphony Orchestra
(computer, software); ARC of Oneida
County (computer); Greater Community
Food Resources (software); Oneida
County Community Action Agency (copy
machine); Legal Aid Society (computer)

Grants awarded to organizations located
in Oneida and Herkimer Counties.

Typical grant range: $5,000 to $25,000

320
Margaret L. Wendt Foundation
40 Fountain Plaza, Suite 277
Buffalo, NY 14202
(716) 855-2146

Buffalo Museum of Science; Home Day
Care Provider (computer); Multiple
Sclerosis Association (software)

Grants awarded to organizations located
in the Buffalo vicinity.

Typical grant range: $3,000 to $30,000

321
Western New York Foundation
Main Seneca Building, Suite 1402
237 Main Street
Buffalo, NY 14203
(716) 847-6440

Arcade Free Library (software); Buffalo
and Erie County Public Library
(microfiche cards); Health Association of
Niagara County (computer, printer)

Typical grant range: $2,500 to $20,000

NORTH CAROLINA

322
**Kathleen Price and Joseph M. Bryan
Family Foundation**
One North Pointe, Suite 170
3101 N. Elm Street
Greensboro, NC 27408
(910) 288-5455

Secondary schools (computer training);
Chowan College (high-tech equipment for
graphic communications department)

Grants awarded to organizations located
in North Carolina.

Typical grant range: $5,000 to $35,000

323
Burroughs Wellcome Fund
4709 Creekstone Drive, Suite 100
Morrisville, NC 27560
(919) 991-5100

Higher education (computer science,
mathematics, science)

Typical grant range: $3,000 to $60,000

324
Cannon Foundation, Inc.
P.O. Box 548
Concord, NC 28026
(704) 786-8216

Science Museums of Wilson; Warren Wilson College (building funds for a science center)

Grants awarded to organizations located in North Carolina, with an emphasis in Cabarrus County.

Typical grant range: $15,000 to $65,000

325
Community Foundation of Henderson County, Inc.
Fourth Avenue and Main Street
P.O. Box 1108
Hendersonville, NC 28793
(704) 697-6224

Visually impaired (high-tech equipment); performing arts (computer, software); Flat Rock Playhouse (computer); Dispute Settlement Center (computer)

Grants awarded to organizations located in Henderson County.

Typical grant range: $250 to $5,000

326
Community Foundation of Western North Carolina, Inc.
14 College Street
Asheville, NC 28801
(704) 254-4960

Museum (computer project); abused children (computer); Alzheimer's Association (computer); Asheville City Schools Foundation (computer)

Grants awarded to organizations located in western North Carolina.

327
Duke Endowment
100 N. Tryon Street, Suite 3500
Charlotte, NC 28202
(704) 376-0291

Duke University Medical Center (computer); Duke University-School of the Environment (laboratory equipment); Duke University-Institutional Research and Planning (computer, software)

328
Duke Power Company Foundation
422 South Church Street
Charlotte, NC 28242
(704) 373-7039

North Carolina School of Science and Mathematics; Roper Mountain Science Center

Grants awarded to organizations located in areas of company operations (Duke Power Company).

Typical grant range: $500 to $10,000

329
First Union Foundation
Two First Union
Charlotte, NC 28288

North Carolina School of Science and Mathematics; National Science Center; Science and Technology Museum

Typical grant range: $500 to $12,000

330
Foundation for the Carolinas
P.O. Box 34769
Charlotte, NC 28234
(704) 376-9541

Carolina Computer Access Center

Grants awarded to organizations located in North Carolina and South Carolina.

331
Foundation of Greater Greensboro, Inc.
100 S. Elm Street, Suite 307
Greensboro, NC 27401
(910) 379-9100

Cultural organizations (computer)

Grants awarded to organizations located in the Greensboro vicinity.

332
Glaxo Foundation
Five Moore Drive
Research Triangle Park, NC 27709
(919) 248-2140

Elementary and secondary education
(science, mathematics); North Carolina
School of Science and Mathematics

Grants awarded to organizations located
in North Carolina.

Typical grant range: $20,000 to $100,000

333
John W. and Anna H. Hanes Foundation
c/o Wachovia Bank of North Carolina, N.A.
P.O. Box 3099, MC 31022
Winston-Salem, NC 27150
(910) 770-5274

Health organization (computer)

Grants awarded to organizations located
in North Carolina.

Typical grant range: $2,000 to $22,000

334
Kate B. Reynolds Charitable Trust
128 Reynolda Village
Winston-Salem, NC 27106
(910) 723-1456

Health organization (computer); United
Way (computer)

Grants awarded to organizations located
in North Carolina.

Typical grant range: $25,000 to $75,000

335
Z. Smith Reynolds Foundation, Inc.
101 Reynolda Village
Winston-Salem, NC 27106
(910) 725-7541

North Carolina School of Science and
Mathematics; Training for Science
Teachers; Science Stars (mathematics,
science project for grades 3 through 6)

Grants awarded to organizations located
in North Carolina.

Typical grant range: $15,000 to $30,000

336
Triangle Community Foundation
100 Park Offices, Suite 209
P.O. Box 12834
Research Triangle Park, NC 27709
(919) 549-9840

Lincoln Community Health Center
(computer)

Grants awarded to organizations located
in Durham, Orange, and Wake Counties.

337
Winston-Salem Foundation
310 W. Fourth Street, Suite 229
Winston-Salem, NC 27101
(910) 725-2382

Social welfare (computer training);
Science Society

Grants awarded to organizations located
in Forsyth County.

Typical grant range: $1,000 to $25,000

OHIO

338
Akron Community Foundation
Society Building, Suite 900
159 S. Main Street
Akron, OH 44308
(216) 376-8522

Cultural organizations (high-tech office
equipment); Battered Women's Shelter
(computer); Our Lady of the Elms
Schools (computer); Western Reserve
Legal Services (computer)

Most grants awarded to organizations
located in the Akron vicinity.

Typical grant range: $1,000 to $20,000

339
Akron Jaycee Foundation
1745 W. Market Street
Akron, OH 44313
(216) 867-8055

Elderly (computer); health organization
(high-tech office equipment); Interfaith
Caregivers (computer, printer)

Grants awarded to organizations located
in Akron.

Typical grant range: $1,000 to $4,000

340
Ashtabula Foundation, Inc.
c/o Society National Bank
4717 Main Avenue
Ashtabula, OH 44004
(216) 992-6818

Ashtabula County Genealogical Society
(printer, microfiche reader); Homesafe
(software, copy machine)

Grants awarded to organizations located
in Ashtabula.

341
**Elsie and Harry Baumker Charitable
Foundation, Inc.**
2828 Barrington Drive
Toledo, OH 43606
(419) 535-6969

Health organizations (high-tech office
equipment)

Grants awarded to organizations located
in Ohio, with an emphasis in Toledo.

Typical grant range: $500 to $7,000

342
William Bingham Foundation
21010 Center Ridge Road, Suite 801
Cleveland, OH 44116
(216) 781-3275

Washington College (computer)

Typical grant range: $5,000 to $40,000

343
**Eva L. and Joseph M. Bruening
Foundation**
1422 Euclid Avenue, Suite 627
Cleveland, OH 44115
(216) 621-2632

Benedictine Order of Cleveland
(computer project)

Grants awarded to organizations located
in the Cleveland vicinity.

Typical grant range: $5,000 to $75,000

344
Cleveland Foundation
1422 Euclid Avenue, Suite 1400
Cleveland, OH 44115
(216) 861-3810

Alcoholism Services of Cleveland
(computer project); Cleveland Heights-
University Heights City School
(mathematics department)

Grants awarded to organizations located
in the Cleveland vicinity.

Typical grant range: $1,000 to $75,000

345
**Columbus Foundation and Affiliated
Organizations**
1234 E. Broad Street
Columbus, OH 43205
(614) 251-4000

Columbus Public Schools (computers for
visual arts department); Ohio Dominican
College (computer project for students
with special needs)

Grants awarded to organizations located
in the Columbus vicinity.

346
**Community Foundation of Greater
Lorain County**
1865 N. Ridge Road East, Suite A
Lorain, OH 44055
(216) 277-0142

Public school system (science department)

Grants awarded to organizations located
in the Lorain County vicinity.

Typical grant range: $1,500 to $12,000

347
Coshocton Foundation
P.O. Box 15
Coshocton, OH 43812
(614) 622-0010

Educational Computer Consortium of Ohio

Grants awarded to organizations located in Coshocton County.

348
Dayton Foundation
2100 Kettering Tower
Dayton, OH 45423
(513) 222-0410

Technology Resource Center (computer, software for people who are visually impaired)

Many grants awarded to organizations located in the Dayton vicinity.

349
Eaton Charitable Fund
Eaton Corporation
Eaton Center
Cleveland, OH 44114
(216) 523-4822

Higher education (science and engineering)

Grants awarded to organizations located in areas of company operations (Eaton Corp.).

Typical grant range: $1,000 to $8,000

350
GAR Foundation
50 S. Main Street
P.O. Box 1500
Akron, OH 44309
(216) 376-5300

West Holmes Local School District (computer, software); School for Girls (computer, computer training); Oberlin College (building funds for the physics laboratory)

Most grants awarded to organizations located in the Akron vicinity.

Typical grant range: $10,000 to $75,000

351
Gould Inc. Foundation
35129 Curtis Blvd.
Eastlake, OH 44094
(216) 953-5000

Higher education (science, engineering)

Grants awarded to organizations located in areas of company operations (Gould Inc.).

Typical grant range: $1,000 to $3,000

352
Greater Cincinnati Foundation
425 Walnut Street, Suite 1110
Cincinnati, OH 45202
(513) 241-2880

Cincinnati Speech and Hearing Center (computer, software); Radio Reading Services (computer); Junior League of Cincinnati (copy machine)

Grants awarded to organizations located in the Cincinnati vicinity.

353
H.C.S. Foundation
1801 E. 9th Street, Suite 1035
Cleveland, OH 44114
(216) 781-3502

Baldwin Wallace College (computer, software for mathematics department)

Grants awarded to organizations located in Ohio.

Typical grant range: $20,000 to $200,000

354
Hoover Foundation
101 E. Maple Street
North Canton, OH 44720
(216) 499-9200

Public library (computer); elderly (computer); Visiting Nurse Society (computer)

Most grants awarded to organizations located in Stark County.

Typical grant range: $10,000 to $80,000

355
Martha Holden Jennings Foundation
710 Halle Building
1228 Euclid Avenue
Cleveland, OH 44115
(216) 589-5700

Xenia City Schools (mathematics department); Madison Board of Education (Computer Assisted Mathematics Program)

Grants awarded to organizations located in Ohio.

Typical grant range: $2,000 to $20,000

356
Kettering Fund
1440 Kettering Tower
Dayton, OH 45423
(513) 228-1021

International Institute for Assistive Technology; GMI Engineering and Management Institute

Typical grant range: $5,000 to $30,000

357
Lubrizol Foundation
29400 Lakeland Blvd., Suite 53A
Wickliffe, OH 44092

Higher education (science, engineering); Lakeland Area Science Teachers

Grants awarded to organizations located in areas of company operations (The Lubrizol Corp.).

Typical grant range: $1,000 to $11,000

358
Charles Moerlein Foundation
c/o Fifth Third Bank
Dept. 00864
Cincinnati, OH 45263
(513) 579-6034

Learning Center (computer); Catholic Social Services (computer); Council on World Affairs (computer)

Grants awarded to organizations located in the Cincinnati vicinity.

Typical grant range: $7,000 to $15,000

359
Nord Family Foundation
347 Midway Blvd., Suite 312
Elyria, OH 44035
(216) 324-2822

American Indian Science and Engineering Society; Musicians Using Systems Incorporating Computers (after school program to improve reading, writing, and mathematics skills)

Grants awarded to organizations located in Cuyahoga and Lorain Counties.

Typical grant range: $10,000 to $50,000

360
Elisabeth Severance Prentiss Foundation
c/o National City Bank
P.O. Box 5756
Cleveland, OH 44101
(216) 575-2760

Neighborhood Health Care (computer)

Grants awarded to organizations located in the Cleveland vicinity.

361
Reeves Foundation
232-4 W. Third Street
P.O. Box 441
Dover, OH 44622
(216) 364-4660

Police Department/Fire Department (communication equipment); County Health Department (radio equipment)

Grants awarded to organizations located in Ohio, with an emphasis in Dover.

362
Reinberger Foundation
27600 Chagrin Blvd.
Cleveland, OH 44122
(216) 292-2790

West Denison Baseball League (computer)

Most grants awarded to organizations located in the Cleveland and Columbus vicinities.

Typical grant range: $10,000 to $80,000

363

Helen Steiner Rice Foundation
221 E. Fourth Street, Suite 2100, Atrium 2
P.O. Box 0236
Cincinnati, OH 45201
(513) 451-9241

University of Cincinnati-College of DAAP
(computer)

Grants awarded to organizations located in
Lorain, Ohio and the Cincinnati vicinity.

Typical grant range: $3,000 to $9,000

364

Fran and Warren Rupp Foundation
40 Sturges Avenue
Mansfield, OH 44902

St. Peter's School (computer laboratory);
MRM-CAP Harmony House (computer)

Typical grant range: $2,000 to $25,000

365

Josephine S. Russell Charitable Trust
PNC Bank, Ohio, N.A.
P.O. Box 1198
Cincinnati, OH 45201
(513) 651-8377

Birthright of Cincinnati (copy machine);
Urban League of Greater Cincinnati
(computer training); Ensemble Theater
of Cincinnati (computer); McAuley High
School (software); Cincinnati Playhouse
in the Park (computer)

Grants awarded to organizations located
in the Cincinnati vicinity.

Typical grant range: $3,000 to $12,000

366

Jacob G. Schmidlapp Trust No. 1
c/o The Fifth Third Bank
Dept. 00864, Foundation Office
Cincinnati, OH 45263
(513) 579-6034

Coalition for People with Disabilities
(computer); Dominican Sisters (computer);
St. Joseph School (computer); Women's
Crisis Center (computer)

Grants awarded to organizations located
in the Cincinnati vicinity.

Typical grant range: $5,000 to $60,000

367

Jacob G. Schmidlapp Trust No. 2
c/o The Fifth Third Bank
Dept. 00864
Cincinnati, OH 45263
(513) 579-6034

Computer grants; secondary education;
health organizations

Grants awarded to organizations located
in the Cincinnati vicinity.

Typical grant range: $5,000 to $25,000

368

Stark County Foundation
The Saxton House
331 Market Avenue South
Canton, OH 44702
(216) 454-3426

Stark County District Library (computer
training for children and young adults)

Grants awarded to organizations located
in Stark County.

Typical grant range: $3,000 to $20,000

369

Frank M. Tait Foundation
Courthouse Plaza, S.W., 5th Floor
Dayton, OH 45402
(513) 222-2401

United Health Services (computer, printer)

Grants awarded to organizations located
in Montgomery County.

Typical grant range: $1,000 to $15,000

370

Troy Foundation
c/o Star Bank, N.A.
910 W. Main Street
Troy, OH 45373
(513) 332-8343

St. Patrick's School (copy machine)

Grants awarded to organizations located
in the Troy vicinity.

371
TRW Foundation
1900 Richmond Road
Cleveland, OH 44124
(216) 291-7166

Higher education (computer science, mathematics, science, engineering); Ohio Academy of Science

Grants awarded to organizations located in areas of company operations (TRW, Inc.), with an emphasis in Cleveland.

Typical grant range: $5,000 to $35,000

OKLAHOMA

372
Mary K. Ashbrook Foundation for El Reno, Oklahoma
P.O. Box 627
El Reno, OK 73036

Public Schools (CD-ROM program); college (computer laboratory); Fire Department (computer)

Grants awarded to organizations located in El Reno.

Typical grant range: $1,000 to $15,000

373
Harris Foundation, Inc.
6403 N.W. Grand Blvd., Suite 211
Oklahoma City, OK 73116
(405) 848-3371

Social welfare (computer); Northwest Oklahoma Pastoral Care (computer); American Red Cross (high-tech office equipment)

Grants awarded to organizations located in Oklahoma.

Typical grant range: $1,000 to $20,000

374
McCasland Foundation
P.O. Box 400
McCasland Building
Duncan, OK 73534
(405) 252-5580

Science and Arts Museum; Cameron University (equipment for the science department)

Most grants awarded to organizations located in Oklahoma.

Typical grant range: $2,000 to $65,000

375
Samuel Roberts Noble Foundation, Inc.
P.O. Box 2180
2510 State Highway 199 East
Ardmore, OK 73402
(405) 223-5810

Higher education (computer laboratory, scientific equipment); Oklahoma Department of Education (workshop for science teachers)

Most grants awarded to organizations located in Oklahoma.

Typical grant range: $10,000 to $125,000

376
Phillips Petroleum Foundation, Inc.
16 C4 Phillips Building
Bartlesville, OK 74004
(918) 661-6248

Oklahoma Engineering Foundation; University of Tulsa (engineering)

Grants awarded to organizations located in areas of company operations (Phillips Petroleum).

Typical grant range: $1,000 to $20,000

377
Presbyterian Health Foundation
711 Stanton L. Young Blvd., Suite 604
Oklahoma City, OK 73104

Oklahoma Center for the Advancement of Science and Technology; Oklahoma School of Science and Mathematics

Grants awarded to organizations located in Oklahoma.

378
Sarkeys Foundation
116 S. Peters, Suite 219
Norman, OK 73069
(405) 364-3703

Performing arts (copy machine);
American Diabetes Association
(computer); Mount St. Mary High
School (computer)

Grants awarded to organizations located
in Oklahoma.

Typical grant range: $5,000 to $80,000

379
Williams Companies Foundation, Inc.
P.O. Box 2400
Tulsa, OK 74172
(918) 588-2106

Oklahoma School of Science and
Mathematics; Sand Springs Public
Schools (science education); University
of Missouri (Center for Computer-Aided
Research); Tulsa Junior College
Foundation (Computer Challenge for
Tulsa students); Community Service
Council (computer)

Grants awarded to organizations located
in areas of company operations (The
Williams Companies, Inc.), with an
emphasis in Tulsa.

Typical grant range: $5,000 to $30,000

OREGON

380
Carpenter Foundation
711 E. Main Street, Suite 10
P.O. Box 816
Medford, OR 97501
(503) 772-5851

Disabled (high-tech office equipment);
Oregon Legal Services Corporation (copy
machine)

Grants awarded to organizations located
in Jackson and Josephine Counties.

Typical grant range: $2,000 to $15,000

381
Collins Foundation
1618 S.W. First Avenue, Suite 305
Portland, OR 97201
(503) 227-7171

Oregon Donor Program (computer);
Coquille Indian Tribe (computer for the
library); Metro Crisis Intervention
(computer project); YWCA (computer
project); Linfield College-Arts and
Humanities Department (computer)

Grants awarded to organizations located
in Oregon.

Typical grant range: $5,000 to $100,000

382
Ford Family Foundation
c/o Roseburg Forest Products Co.
P.O. Box 1088
Roseburg, OR 97470

Elementary school (automate library);
Oregon Museum of Science and Industry

Typical grant range: $2,000 to $60,000

383
Intel Foundation
JF3-127
5200 N.E. Elam Young Parkway
Hillsboro, OR 97124
(503) 264-1858

Higher education (computer science,
engineering); American Indian Science
and Engineering Society; Oregon
Museum of Science and Industry
(computer exhibit)

Grants awarded to organizations located
in areas of company operations (Intel
Corporation).

Typical grant range: $3,000 to $40,000

384

Meyer Memorial Trust
1515 S.W. Fifth Avenue, Suite 500
Portland, OR 97201
(503) 228-5512

High School (computer laboratory);
Community Health Center (computer,
software); Aslan Counseling Center
(computer); Battered Persons' Advocacy
(computer); Jackson County Child Abuse
Task Force (computer, copy machine)

Most grants awarded to organizations
located in Oregon.

385

Oregon Community Foundation
621 S.W. Morrison, Suite 725
Portland, OR 97205
(503) 227-6846

Oregon Graduate Institute of Science and
Technology

Grants awarded to organizations located
in Oregon.

Typical grant range: $1,500 to $25,000

386

Tektronix Foundation
P.O. Box 1000, M.S. 63-813
Wilsonville, OR 97070
(503) 685-4030

Higher education (engineering, science);
Museum of Science and Industry

Grants awarded to organizations located
in Oregon.

Typical grant range: $12,000 to $25,000

387

Rose E. Tucker Charitable Trust
900 S.W. Fifth Avenue, 24th Floor
Portland, OR 97204
(503) 224-3380

Hospital (computer); Oregon Museum of
Science and Industry

Most grants awarded to organizations
located in the Portland vicinity.

Typical grant range: $2,000 to $11,000

PENNSYLVANIA

388

Air Products Foundation
7201 Hamilton Blvd.
Allentown, PA 18195
(610) 481-6349

Higher education (computer science,
engineering, science)

Grants awarded to organizations located
in areas of company operations (Air
Products and Chemicals, Inc.).

Typical grant range: $500 to $9,000

389

Alcoa Foundation
2202 Alcoa Building
425 Sixth Avenue
Pittsburgh, PA 15219
(412) 553-2348

Higher education (computer science,
engineering, mathematics, science);
Community School District (science,
mathematics)

Grants awarded to organizations located
in areas of company operations
(Aluminum Co. of America).

Typical grant range: $1,000 to $15,000

390

Allegheny Foundation
Three Mellon Bank Center
525 William Penn Place, Suite 3900
Pittsburgh, PA 15219
(412) 392-2900

Higher education (computer science);
Greensburg Hempfield Library
(automation)

Most grants awarded to organizations
located in western Pennsylvania.

Typical grant range: $5,000 to $70,000

391

Annenberg Foundation
St. Davids Center
150 Radnor-Chester Road, Suite A-200
St. Davids, PA 19087
(610) 341-9066

Teachers Academy for Mathematics and
Science; Philadelphia Regional
Introduction for Minorities to Engineering

Typical grant range: $20,000 to $300,000

392

Barra Foundation, Inc.
8200 Flourtown Avenue, Suite 12
Wyndmoor, PA 19038
(215) 233-5115

Philadelphia College of Textiles and
Science (computer project)

Most grants awarded to organizations
located in the Philadelphia vicinity.

Typical grant range: $500 to $10,000

393

Bayer Foundation
One Mellon Center
500 Grant Street
Pittsburgh, PA 15219
(412) 394-6725

Higher education (science; engineering
program for minorities); Carnegie Mellon
University (computer laboratory)

Typical grant range: $1,000 to $15,000

394

Buhl Foundation
Four Gateway Center, Room 1325
Pittsburgh, PA 15222
(412) 566-2711

Pittsburgh Supercomputing Center;
Northside Common Ministries
(computer); Extra Mile Education
Foundation (computer); Pace School
(computer training for people with
disabilities)

Most grants awarded to organizations
located in the Pittsburgh vicinity.

Typical grant range: $5,000 to $75,000

395

**E. Rhodes and Leona B. Carpenter
Foundation**
c/o Joseph A. O'Connor, Jr., Morgan,
Lewis & Bockius
2000 One Logan Square
Philadelphia, PA 19103
(215) 963-5212

Richmond Symphony (computer);
Russellville Independent School
(computer)

Typical grant range: $10,000 to $85,000

396

CIGNA Foundation
One Liberty Place
1650 Market Street
Philadelphia, PA 19192
(215) 761-6055

Middle school (computer center); Franklin
Institute Science Museum and
Planetarium

Typical grant range: $3,000 to $40,000

397

Connelly Foundation
One Tower Bridge, Suite 1450
West Conshohocken, PA 19428
(215) 834-3222

Philadelphia Protestant Home for the
Aged (computer project); Catholic School
(software)

Typical grant range: $2,000 to $50,000

398

Eden Hall Foundation
600 Grant Street
Pittsburgh, PA 15219
(412) 642-6697

Computer literacy project; AIDS Task
Force (computer)

Typical grant range: $15,000 to $125,000

399
Erie Community Foundation
127 W. Sixth Street
Erie, PA 16501
(814) 454-0843

Penn Lake Girl Scouts (computer, software); G.R.O.W. (computer)

Grants awarded to organizations located in Erie County.

Typical grant range: $2,000 to $15,000

400
Howard Heinz Endowment
30 CNG Tower
625 Liberty Avenue
Pittsburgh, PA 15222
(412) 281-5777

Technology Development and Education Corporation; Kiskiminetas Springs School (laboratory for the science department)

Grants awarded to organizations located in Pennsylvania.

Typical grant range: $50,000 to $300,000

401
Vira I. Heinz Endowment
30 CNG Tower
625 Liberty Avenue
Pittsburgh, PA 15222
(412) 281-5777

La Roche College (program to enhance science education in elementary, middle and high schools); Carnegie Mellon University (interactive video library technology project)

Most grants awarded to organizations located in the Pittsburgh vicinity.

Typical grant range: $15,000 to $200,000

402
Hillman Foundation, Inc.
2000 Grant Building
Pittsburgh, PA 15219
(412) 338-3466

Deaf (high-tech equipment); American Red Cross (computer file server); Community College of Allegheny County-Institute of Advanced Technology (computer, software)

Most grants awarded to organizations located in the Pittsburgh vicinity.

Typical grant range: $5,000 to $75,000

403
T. James Kavanagh Foundation
57 Northwood Road
Newtown Square, PA 19073
(215) 356-0743

County Day School of The Sacred Heart (computer); MBF Computer Center (computer training); Lansdowne Friends School (computer)

Most grants awarded to Catholic organizations.

Typical grant range: $500 to $3,000

404
Josiah W. and Bessie H. Kline Foundation, Inc.
42 Kline Village
Harrisburg, PA 17104
(717) 232-0266

Scientific research; West Shore Public Library (computer)

Grants awarded to organizations located in south central Pennsylvania.

Typical grant range: $2,000 to $25,000

405
Lehigh Valley Community Foundation
961 Marcon Blvd., Suite 110
Allentown, PA 18103
(215) 266-4284

AIDS Service Center (copy machine)

Grants awarded to organizations located in Lehigh and Northampton Counties.

Typical grant range: $500 to $10,000

406
Philip M. McKenna Foundation, Inc.
P.O. Box 186
Latrobe, PA 15650
(412) 537-6900

Saint Vincent College (automate library)

Typical grant range: $3,000 to $65,000

407
R.K. Mellon Family Foundation
One Mellon Bank Center
500 Grant Street, Suite 4106
Pittsburgh, PA 15219
(412) 392-2800

Research Science Institute; Madison House (computer, software)

Grants awarded to organizations located in western Pennsylvania.

Typical grant range: $5,000 to $35,000

408
Richard King Mellon Foundation
One Mellon Bank Center
500 Grant Street, 41st Floor
Pittsburgh, PA 15219
(412) 392-2800

Youth organization (computer); Coalition for Christian Outreach (computer)

Most grants awarded to organizations located in Pittsburgh.

Typical grant range: $40,000 to $250,000

409
William Penn Foundation
1630 Locust Street
Philadelphia, PA 19103
(215) 988-1830

Higher education (mathematics, science, engineering, minorities); Public Library of Phoenixville (automation project)

Typical grant range: $5,000 to $125,000

410
Pew Charitable Trusts
One Commerce Square
2005 Market Street, Suite 1700
Philadelphia, PA 19103
(215) 575-9050

Higher education (mathematics and science workshop for high school teachers); University of Pennsylvania-Center for Solid Waste Systems and Technology (computer project)

411
Dr. & Mrs. Arthur William Phillips Charitable Trust
229 Elm Street
P.O. Box 316
Oil City, PA 16301
(215) 676-2736

American Cancer Society (computer, software); Oil City Area School District (laptop computer); VNA (computer); Clarion Free Library (copy machine)

412
Pittsburgh Foundation
One PPG Place, 30th Floor
Pittsburgh, PA 15222
(412) 391-5122

Higher education (science, engineering); Pittsburgh Public Theater Corp. (computer project); Goodwill Industries (computer training); Community Technical Assistance Center (computer project)

Grants awarded to organizations located in the Pittsburgh vicinity.

Typical grant range: $5,000 to $50,000

413
PPG Industries Foundation
One PPG Place
Pittsburgh, PA 15272
(412) 434-2962

Buhl Science Center; National Action Council for Minorities in Engineering

Grants awarded to organizations located in areas of company operations (PPG Industries, Inc.), with an emphasis in Pittsburgh.

414
Rockwell International Corporation Trust
625 Liberty Avenue
Pittsburgh, PA 15222
(412) 565-5803

Higher education (engineering, science, mathematics)

Grants awarded to organizations located in areas of company operations (Rockwell International Corporation).

415
Ethel Sergeant Clark Smith Memorial Fund
c/o CoreStates Bank, N.A.
P.O. Box 7618, FC 1-3-9-74
Philadelphia, PA 19101
(215) 973-3704

Alcoholism and Addictions Council (computer project); Recording for the Blind (computer)

Grants awarded to organizations located in Delaware County.

Typical grant range: $5,000 to $40,000

416
Hoxie Harrison Smith Foundation
210 Fairlamb Avenue
Havertown, PA 19083
(610) 446-4651

Inglish House Foundation (computer)

417
Harry C. Trexler Trust
33 S. Seventh Street, Suite 205
Allentown, PA 18101
(215) 434-9645

Youth organization (computer); Literacy Center (software); Lehigh County Community College (computer for the library)

Grants awarded to organizations located in Lehigh County.

Typical grant range: $12,000 to $30,000

418
USX Foundation, Inc.
600 Grant Street, Room 727
Pittsburgh, PA 15219
(412) 433-5237

Higher education (computer science, engineering, science)

Grants awarded to organizations located in areas of company operations (USX Corporation).

Typical grant range: $3,000 to $40,000

419
Westinghouse Foundation
Westinghouse Electric Corporation
11 Stanwix Street
Pittsburgh, PA 15222
(412) 642-6033

Higher education (computer science, engineering, science); Pittsburgh High Technology Council

Grants awarded to organizations located in areas of company operations (Westinghouse Electric Corporation).

Typical grant range: $2,000 to $60,000

PUERTO RICO

420
Puerto Rico Community Foundation
Royal Bank Center Building, Suite 1417
Hato Rey, PR 00917
(809) 751-3822

Higher education (computer science, engineering, science)

Grants awarded to organizations located in Puerto Rico.

Typical grant range: $5,000 to $35,000

RHODE ISLAND

421
Champlin Foundations
410 S. Main Street
Providence, RI 02903
(401) 421-3719

Public Library (computer); Roger
Williams Park Museum of Natural History
(computer)

Grants awarded to organizations located
in Rhode Island.

Typical grant range: $10,000 to $100,000

422
Edward E. Ford Foundation
199 Wickenden Street
Providence, RI 02903
(401)751-2966

Columbus School for Girls (computer);
Covenant of Sacred Heart (computer,
software); Charles Wright Academy
(computer, software); Episcopal High
School (computers, monitors)

Grants awarded to independent secondary
schools who are members of the National
Association of Independent Schools.

Typical grant range: $20,000 to $50,000

423
Ida Ballou Littlefield Memorial Trust
1500 Fleet Center
Providence, RI 02903
(401) 274-2000

Save the Bay (copy machine); Insight
(computer)

Typical grant range: $5,000 to $20,000

SOUTH CAROLINA

424
**Central Carolina Community
Foundation**
P.O. Box 11222
Columbia, SC 29211
(803) 254-5601

Newberry County Career Center (software
for nursing program)

Typical grant range: $1,000 to $5,000

425
Hamrick Mills Foundation, Inc.
P.O. Box 48
Gaffney, SC 29342

Cherokee County Public Library
(computer, microfiche machine)

Grants awarded to organizations located
in Cherokee County.

Typical grant range: $500 to $6,000

426
Self Foundation
P.O. Drawer 1017
Greenwood, SC 29648
(803) 941-4036

Higher education (science department,
computer network for campus); Public
Library (computer)

Grants awarded to organizations located
in South Carolina, with an emphasis in the
Greenwood vicinity.

Typical grant range: $5,000 to $50,000

427
Spartanburg County Foundation
320 E. Main Street
Spartanburg, SC 29302
(803) 582-0138

Spartanburg Day School (computer)

Grants awarded to organizations located
in Spartanburg County.

Typical grant range: $1,000 to $12,000

428
Springs Foundation, Inc.
P.O. Drawer 460
Lancaster, SC 29721
(803) 286-2196

Junior high school (science department);
Heath Springs Elementary School
(computer project)

Grants awarded to organizations located
in Lancaster County and Chester and Fort
Mill, South Carolina.

Typical grant range: $3,000 to $30,000

TENNESSEE

429
HCA Foundation
One Park Plaza, P.O. Box 550
Nashville, TN 37202
(615) 320-2165

Family and Children's Service
(computer); League for the Hearing
Impaired (computer); Leukemia Society
(fax machine); March of Dimes (copy
machine)

Most grants awarded to organizations
located in Nashville.

Typical grant range: $1,000 to $25,000

430
Maclellan Foundation, Inc.
Provident Building, Suite 501
Chattanooga, TN 37402
(615) 755-1366

Ministry (computer); Latin American
Association (computer)

Most grants awarded to Protestant related
organizations.

Grants awarded to organizations located
in the Chattanooga vicinity.

Typical grant range: $30,000 to $100,000

431
R.J. Maclellan Charitable Trust
Provident Building, Suite 501
Chattanooga, TN 37402
(615) 755-1366

Crown Ministries, Inc. (computer)

Most grants awarded to Protestant related
organizations.

Most grants awarded to organizations
located in Chattanooga.

Typical grant range: $15,000 to $125,000

432
Tonya Memorial Foundation
American National Bank & Trust Co.
736 Market Street
Chattanooga, TN 37402

Hospice (computer)

Grants awarded to organizations located
in Chattanooga.

Typical grant range: $5,000 to $200,000

433
Robert Lee Weiss Foundation
c/o First Tennessee Bank, N.A.
Trust Division
800 South Gay Street
Knoxville, TN 37995

Habitat for Humanity (software)

Most grants awarded to organizations
located in the Knoxville vicinity.

Typical grant range: $4,000 to $20,000

TEXAS

434
Brown Foundation, Inc.
P.O. Box 130646
Houston, TX 77219
(713) 523-6867

Higher education (engineering,
minorities); Science Engineering Fair

Grants awarded to organizations located
in Texas, with an emphasis in Houston.

Typical grant range: $15,000 to $120,000

435
Burkitt Foundation
5847 San Felipe, Suite 4290
Houston, TX 77057
(713) 780-7638

Incarnate Word College (computer, software)

Typical grant range: $1,000 to $7,000

436
Amon G. Carter Foundation
500 W. Seventh Street, Suite 1212
P.O. Box 1036
Fort Worth, TX 76101
(817) 332-2783

Center for Computer Assistance to the Disabled

Grants awarded to organizations located in the Fort Worth vicinity.

Typical grant range: $2,000 to $35,000

437
Community Foundation of Abilene
500 Chestnut, Suite 1509
P.O. Box 1001
Abilene, TX 79604
(915) 676-3883

Youth organization (computer, software); museum (high-tech office equipment); Serenity House (computer, printer); Food Bank (computer, software)

Grants awarded to organizations located in the Abilene vicinity.

Typical grant range: $1,000 to $12,000

438
Compaq Computer Foundation
P.O. Box 692000-040511
Houston, TX 77269
(713) 374-0527

Science Engineering Fair; National Society of Professional Engineers Educational Foundation

Most grants awarded to organizations located in Houston.

Typical grant range: $5,000 to $25,000

439
Cullen Foundation
601 Jefferson, 40th Floor
Houston, TX 77002
(713) 651-8837

Hospital (computer project); Kinkaid School (mathematics, science)

Grants awarded to organizations located in Texas, with an emphasis in Houston.

Typical grant range: $75,000 to $350,000

440
Davidson Family Charitable Foundation
70 N.E. Loop 410, Suite 550
San Antonio, TX 78216

Center for Computer Assistance to the Disabled

Grants awarded to organizations located in Texas.

441
James R. Dougherty, Jr. Foundation
P.O. Box 640
Beeville, TX 78104
(512) 358-3560

St. Joseph Academy (science laboratory)

Grants awarded to organizations located in Texas.

Typical grant range: $1,000 to $4,000

442
Dresser Foundation, Inc.
P.O. Box 718
Dallas, TX 75221
(214) 740-6078

Science Engineering Fair; School of Engineering

Grants awarded to organizations located in areas of company operations (Dresser Industries, Inc.).

Typical grant range: $1,000 to $15,000

443

Exxon Education Foundation
225 E. John W. Carpenter Freeway
Irving, TX 75062
(214) 444-1104

Secondary education (mathematics);
higher education (science, mathematics);

Typical grant range: $3,000 to $50,000

444

First Interstate Foundation of Texas
1000 Louisiana Street
P.O. Box 3326, MS No. 584
Houston, TX 77253
(713) 250-1850

Independent School District (computer)

Grants awarded to organizations located
in Texas.

445

Fondren Foundation
7 TCT 37
P.O. Box 2558
Houston, TX 77252
(713) 236-4403

DNA Technology Laboratory; University
of Houston (electronic information
network)

Most grants awarded to organizations
located in Houston.

Typical grant range: $15,000 to $125,000

446

George Foundation
207 S. Third Street
P.O. Drawer C
Richmond, TX 77469
(713) 342-6109

Space Science Educational Foundation for
Tomorrow; Rice University (workshop for
high school mathematics teachers)

Most grants awarded to organizations
located in Ft. Bend County.

Typical grant range: $10,000 to $50,000

447

Halliburton Foundation, Inc.
3600 Lincoln Plaza
500 N. Akard Street
Dallas, TX 75201
(214) 978-2600

Higher education (computer science,
engineering, science); University of
Houston (computer science)

Typical grant range: $5,000 to $30,000

448

**George and Mary Josephine Hamman
Foundation**
910 Travis Street, Suite 1990
Houston, TX 77002
(713) 658-8345

Houston Museum of Natural Science

Grants awarded to organizations located
in Texas.

449

Hillcrest Foundation
c/o NationsBank of Texas, N.A.
Trust Division
P.O. Box 830241
Dallas, TX 75283
(214) 508-1965

Dallas Lighthouse for the Blind (laser
printer); Boys and Girls Club (computer
training)

Grants awarded to organizations located
in Texas, with an emphasis in Dallas.

Typical grant range: $5,000 to $50,000

450

Hoblitzelle Foundation
5956 Sherry Lane, Suite 901
Dallas, TX 75225
(214) 373-0462

Center for Computer Assistance to the
Disabled; American Diabetes Association
(computer project); Bishop Dunne High
School (computer); Fine Arts Chamber
Players (computer); Dallas Public Library
(high-tech project); Schreiner College
(computer); Child Protective Services
(computer)

Grants awarded to organizations located
in Texas, with an emphasis in Dallas.

Typical grant range: $15,000 to $75,000

451

Houston Endowment, Inc.
600 Travis, Suite 6400
Houston, TX 77002
(713) 238-8100

Secondary education (workshop for
physics teachers); North Harris
Montgomery Community College District
Foundation (high-tech equipment for
Geoscience Technology Center)

Grants awarded to organizations located
in Texas, with an emphasis in Houston.

Typical grant range: $5,000 to $250,000

452

**M.G. and Lillie A. Johnson
Foundation, Inc.**
P.O. Box 2269
Victoria, TX 77902
(512) 575-7970

Hospice of South Texas (computer,
software); County Medical Services
(computer); Palmer Drug Abuse Program
(computer); South Texas Children's Home
(computer, software); Yoakum
Community Hospital (communication
equipment)

Grants awarded to organizations located
in Texas.

Typical grant range: $20,000 to $100,000

453

Harris and Eliza Kempner Fund
P.O. Box 119
Galveston, TX 77553
(409) 762-1603

Computer grants; cultural organizations;
social welfare; health organizations

Grants awarded to organizations located
in Galveston.

Typical grant range: $1,500 to $8,500

454

Meadows Foundation, Inc.
Wilson Historic Block
3003 Swiss Avenue
Dallas, TX 75204
(214) 826-9431

Del City Independent School District
(technology center); Southwestern
Christian College (building funds for the
science department)

Grants awarded to organizations located
in Texas.

Typical grant range: $25,000 to $80,000

455

Moody Foundation
2302 Postoffice Street, Suite 704
Galveston, TX 77550
(409) 763-5333

Higher education (science, mathematics,
engineering); Nature Conservancy
(computer project)

Grants awarded to organizations located
in Texas.

Typical grant range: $15,000 to $200,000

456

O'Donnell Foundation
100 Crescent Court, Suite 1660
Dallas, TX 75201
(214) 871-5800

Higher education (science, engineering);
South Methodist University (technology
in education program); Dallas Museum of
Art (technology in education program)

Grants awarded to organizations located
in Texas.

457

RGK Foundation
2815 San Gabriel
Austin, TX 78705
(512) 474-9298

Higher education (science); elementary school (science project); Texas College of Osteopathic Medicine (science project for high school minority students)

458

Sid W. Richardson Foundation
309 Main Street
Fort Worth, TX 76102
(817) 336-0494

Center for Computer Assistance to the Disabled; Fort Worth Regional Science Fair; Texas Christian University (science equipment)

Grants awarded to organizations located in Texas.

Typical grant range: $10,000 to $125,000

459

Rockwell Fund, Inc.
1360 Post Oak Blvd., Suite 780
Houston, TX 77056
(713) 629-9022

Disabled (computer); health organizations (high-tech projects); Audubon Society (science program)

Grants awarded to organizations located in Texas, with an emphasis in Houston.

Typical grant range: $10,000 to $25,000

460

San Antonio Area Foundation
530 McCullough, Suite 650
San Antonio, TX 78215
(210) 225-2243

Computer grants; high-tech office equipment; health organizations; hospice; abused women; youth organizations; disabled

Grants awarded to organizations located in the San Antonio vicinity.

Typical grant range: $500 to $15,000

461

Shell Oil Company Foundation
Two Shell Plaza
P.O. Box 2099
Houston, TX 77252
(713) 241-3616

Higher education (computer science, engineering, science); Science Engineering Fair of Houston

Grants awarded to organizations located in areas of company operations (Shell Oil Company).

Typical grant range: $2,000 to $40,000

462

Clara Blackford Smith and W. Aubrey Smith Charitable Foundation
c/o NationsBank of Texas, N.A.
300 W. Main Street
Denison, TX 75020
(903) 415-2317

Grayson County Rehabilitation Center (computer)

Most grants awarded to organizations located in Denison.

463

T.L.L. Temple Foundation
109 Temple Blvd.
Lufkin, TX 75901
(409) 639-5197

Shelbyville Independent School District (technology center); University of Houston-University Park (superconductivity research)

Grants awarded to organizations located in the Deep East Texas Pine Timber Belt.

Typical grant range: $10,000 to $100,000

464

Julia Love Tuschman Foundation
7670 Woodway Drive, Suite 120
Houston, TX 77063
(713) 626-7200

Texas Research Society on Alcoholism (computer, printer); Pyramid House (copy machine)

465
Vale-Asche Foundation
1010 River Oaks Bank Building
2001 Kirby Drive
Houston, TX 77019
(713) 520-7334

Houston Area Women's Center (laptop computer); American Red Cross (satellite equipment); Volunteer Center (computer)

Grants awarded to organizations located in Houston.

Typical grant range: $2,000 to $30,000

466
Robert A. Welch Foundation
4605 Post Oak Place, Suite 200
Houston, TX 77027
(713) 961-9884

Higher education (chemistry research)

Grants awarded to organizations located in Texas.

UTAH

467
George S. and Dolores Dore Eccles Foundation
Deseret Building, 12th Floor
79 S. Main Street
Salt Lake City, UT 84111
(801) 246-5336

Higher education (computer project for the nursing department); Utah Issues (computer)

Most grants awarded to organizations located in Utah.

Typical grant range: $5,000 to $90,000

468
Marriner S. Eccles Foundation
701 Deseret Building
79 S. Main Street
Salt Lake City, UT 84111
(801) 322-0116

Higher education (engineering, science)

Grants awarded to organizations located in Utah.

Typical grant range: $3,000 to $30,000

469
Willard L. Eccles Charitable Foundation
P.O. Box 45385
Salt Lake City, UT 84145
(801) 532-1500

Autism Society (computer)

Grants awarded to organizations located in Utah.

Typical grant range: $5,000 to $75,000

470
Henry W. and Leslie M. Eskuche Charitable Foundation
c/o West One Trust Co.
P.O. Box 3058
Salt Lake City, UT 84110

Westminster College (computer for library)

Grants awarded to organizations located in Utah.

Typical grant range: $1,000 to $10,000

VERMONT

471
Canaan Foundation for Christian Education
R. R. One
P.O. Box 113
Woodstock, VT 05091
(802) 457-3990

Christian School (computer); Campers Crusade for Christ (computer)

Few grants awarded.

472
Lintilhac Foundation
100 Harbor Road
Shelburne, VT 05482
(802) 985-4106

University of Vermont-Dept. of Tech. (interactive video science project)

Typical grant range: $1,000 to $15,000

473
Mortimer R. Proctor Trust
Green Mountain Bank, Trust Dept.
P.O. Box 669
Rutland, VT 05701
(802) 775-2525

Proctor School System (computer)

Grants awarded to organizations located in Proctor, Vermont.

Typical grant range: $2,000 to $20,000

VIRGINIA

474
Beazley Foundation, Inc.
3720 Brighton Street
Portsmouth, VA 23707
(804) 393-1605

Girls Club of Portsmouth (computer)

Typical grant range: $5,000 to $90,000

475
Community Foundation Serving Richmond & Central Virginia
9211 Forest Hill Avenue, Suite 109
Richmond, VA 23235
(804) 330-7400

Science Museum of Virginia; Riverside School (computer and software for students with dyslexia)

Grants awarded to organizations located in the Richmond vicinity and central Virginia.

Typical grant range: $1,000 to $11,000

476
Massey Foundation
P.O. Box 26765
Richmond, VA 23261
(804) 648-2615

Science Museum of Virginia; National Youth Science Camp Foundation

Grants awarded to organizations located in Virginia.

Typical grant range: $1,000 to $30,000

477
Norfolk Foundation
1410 NationsBank Center
Norfolk, VA 23510
(804) 622-7951

Family Services of Tidewater (computer); Medical College of Hampton Roads (computer for the library); Norfolk Academy (computer project); St. Mary's Infant Home (computer project); The Chrysler Museum (computer for the library)

Grants awarded to organizations located in the Norfolk vicinity.

Typical grant range: $15,000 to $50,000

478
Norfolk Southern Foundation
Three Commercial Place
Norfolk, VA 23510
(804) 629-2720

Science Museum of Western Virginia; Davidson College (science department)

Typical grant range: $1,000 to $35,000

479
Mary Morton Parsons Foundation
P.O. Box 85678
Richmond, VA 23285

Science Museum; Mathematics and Science Center

Most grants awarded to organizations located in Richmond.

Typical grant range: $25,000 to $100,000

480
Perry Foundation, Inc.
P.O. Box 558
Charlottesville, VA 22902
(804) 973-9441

Meals on Wheels (computer); Elk Hill Farm (computer laboratory); Piedmont Environmental Council (computer)

Grants awarded to organizations located in Virginia.

Typical grant range: $5,000 to $50,000

481
C.E. Richardson Benevolent Foundation
74 W. Main Street, Room 211
P.O. Box 1120
Pulaski, VA 24301
(703) 980-6628

Literacy Volunteers of America (copy machine)

Typical grant range: $1,000 to $6,000

482
J. Edwin Treakle Foundation, Inc.
P.O. Box 1157
Gloucester, VA 23061
(804) 693-0881

Higher education (science laboratory equipment, audiovisual equipment); School District (computer); Memorial Library (copy machine); Humane Society (computer)

Grants awarded to organizations located in Virginia.

Typical grant range: $1,000 to $7,500

WASHINGTON

483
Ben B. Cheney Foundation, Inc.
1201 Pacific Avenue, Suite 1600
Tacoma, WA 98402
(206) 572-2442

Public television (high-tech projects); youth organizations (computer project); Food Bank (computer); Resource Center for the Handicapped (technology laboratory)

Typical grant range: $2,000 to $45,000

484
Comstock Foundation
819 Washington Trust Financial Center
West 717 Sprague Avenue
Spokane, WA 99204
(509) 747-1527

AIDS Life Link (computer); Cancer Path Services (computer); Eastern Washington Center for the Deaf and Hard of Hearing (computer); Lutheran Social Services (computer); Lilac Blind Foundation (laser printer, laptop computer); Partners for Community Living (fax machine); Women Helping Women Fund (computer, fax machine, copy machine); Spokane Neighborhood Action Program (computer); St. Joseph's Family Center (computer)

Grants awarded to organizations located in Washington.

Typical grant range: $1,000 to $30,000

485
Glaser Foundation, Inc.
P.O. Box 6548
Bellevue, WA 98008

Pacific Science Center

Most grants awarded to organizations located in the King County vicinity.

486
Laird, Norton Foundation
801 Second Avenue, Suite 1300
Seattle, WA 98104
(206) 464-5292

Pacific Science Center Foundation

487
M.J. Murdock Charitable Trust
P.O. Box 1618
Vancouver, WA 98668
(206) 694-8415

Disabled (computer); higher education (science, engineering); Oregon Independent College Foundation (computer project)

Typical grant range: $10,000 to $200,000

488
Seattle Foundation
425 Pike Street, Suite 510
Seattle, WA 98101
(206) 622-2294

Community development (computer);
Korean Community Counseling Center
(computer); Mental Health Center
(computer, printers)

Grants awarded to organizations located
in Seattle.

Typical grant range: $3,000 to $20,000

489
Weyerhaeuser Company Foundation
CH 1F31
Tacoma, WA 98477
(206) 924-3159

Higher education (engineering);
elementary school (computer, software);
Pacific Science Center

Grants awarded to organizations located
in areas of company operations
(Weyerhaeuser Company).

Typical grant range: $3,000 to $15,000

WEST VIRGINIA

490
Beckley Area Foundation, Inc.
P.O. Box 1092
Beckley, WV 25802

Elementary school (computer project);
Episcopal Day School (computer);
Sheltered Workshop (copy machine);
Compassionate Friends (copy machine)

Grants awarded to organizations located
in the Beckley vicinity.

Typical grant range: $500 to $8,000

491
Greater Kanawha Valley Foundation
1426 Kanawha Blvd., East
Charleston, WV 25301
(304) 346-3620

Middle school (science project);
elementary school (high-tech office
equipment); high school (computer);
women (high-tech office equipment);
Goodwill Industries (software)

Grants awarded to organizations located
in the Greater Kanawha Valley.

Typical grant range: $1,000 to $14,000

492
**Parkersburg Area Community
Foundation**
402 Juliana Street
P.O. Box 1762
Parkersburg, WV 26102
(304) 428-4438

Social welfare (computer); Parkersburg
and Wood County Public Library
(computer); West Virginia University
(laser disc machine for Natural Science
and Mathematics Department)

Grants awarded to organizations located
in the Parkersburg vicinity.

Typical grant range: $500 to $4,000

WISCONSIN

493
**Lynde and Harry Bradley
Foundation, Inc.**
777 E. Wisconsin Avenue, Suite 2285
Milwaukee, WI 53202
(414) 291-9915

Milwaukee School of Engineering;
Discovery World Museum of Science,
Economics and Technology

Typical grant range: $20,000 to $125,000

494
Community Foundation for the Fox Valley Region, Inc.
P.O. Box 563
Appleton, WI 54912
(414) 830-1290

Developmentally disabled (computer training); Waupaca High School (software and computer for students with disabilities)

Grants awarded to organizations located in the Fox Valley vicinity.

495
Patrick and Anna M. Cudahy Fund
P.O. Box 11978
Milwaukee, WI 53211
(708) 866-0760

Secondary education (computer training); Office Technology Academy (computer training)

Typical grant range: $3,000 to $25,000

496
Elizabeth Elser Doolittle Charitable Trust No. 1
c/o Foley & Lardner
777 E. Wisconsin Avenue
Milwaukee, WI 53202

Urban Day School (software)

Most grants awarded to organizations located in Wisconsin.

Typical grant range: $1,000 to $8,000

497
Firstar Milwaukee Foundation, Inc.
777 E. Wisconsin Avenue
Milwaukee, WI 53202
(414) 765-4579

Milwaukee Public Library Foundation (computer)

Grants awarded to organizations located in the Milwaukee vicinity.

Typical grant range: $1,000 to $20,000

498
Greater Green Bay Community Foundation
333 Main Street, Suite 177
Green Bay, WI 54301
(414) 432-0800

Big Brothers/Big Sisters (software); Cerebral Palsy, Inc. (software)

Grants awarded to organizations located in the Green Bay vicinity.

499
Madison Community Foundation
615 E. Washington Avenue
Madison, WI 53703
(608) 255-0503

Family Services (computer); Alliance for the Mentally Ill (computer project); South Madison Neighborhood Center (computer project)

Grants awarded to organizations located in the Madison vicinity.

Typical grant range: $1,000 to $25,000

500
Marshall & Ilsley Foundation, Inc.
770 North Water Street
Milwaukee, WI 53202
(414) 765-7835

Milwaukee School of Engineering

Grants awarded to organizations located in Wisconsin.

Typical grant range: $1,000 to $40,000

501
Faye McBeath Foundation
1020 North Broadway
Milwaukee, WI 53202
(414) 272-2626

Youth organization (computer training); Discovery World Museum of Science, Economics and Technology

Grants awarded to organizations located in Wisconsin, with an emphasis in Milwaukee.

Typical grant range: $10,000 to $40,000

502
Milwaukee Foundation
1020 North Broadway
Milwaukee, WI 53202
(414) 272-5805

Youth organization (computer training);
middle school (mathematics department);
disabled (computer project); Milwaukee
Area American Indian Manpower Council
(computer training)

Grants awarded to organizations located
in the Milwaukee vicinity.

Typical grant range: $5,000 to $50,000

503
L.E. Phillips Family Foundation, Inc.
3925 N. Hastings Way
Eau Claire, WI 54703
(715) 839-2139

Secondary education (computer
department)

Typical grant range: $500 to $11,000

504
**Wausau Area Community
Foundation, Inc.**
500 Third Street, Suite 316
Wausau, WI 54403
(715) 845-9555

Secondary education (computer);
Storefront Learning Center (computer for
an alternative high school program)

Grants awarded to organizations located
in the Wausau vicinity.

Typical grant range: $300 to $3,000

Appendix A
The Foundation Center

The Foundation Center is an independent national service organization established by foundations to provide an authoritative source of information on private philanthropic giving. In fulfilling its mission, the Foundation Center disseminates information on private giving through public service programs, publications and through a national network of library reference collections for free public use. The New York, Washington, DC, Atlanta, Cleveland and San Francisco reference collections operated by the Foundation Center offer a wide variety of services and comprehensive collections of information on foundations and grants. The Cooperating Collections are libraries, community foundations and other nonprofit agencies that provide a core collection of Foundation Center publications and a variety of supplementary materials and services in subject areas useful to grantseekers.

Many of the network members make available sets of private foundation information returns (IRS Form 990-PF) for their state and/or neighboring states which are available for public use. A complete set of U.S. foundation returns can be found at the New York and Washington, DC, offices of the Foundation Center. The Atlanta, Cleveland, and San Francisco offices contain IRS Form 990-PF returns for the southeastern, midwestern, and western states, respectively.

Those collections marked with a bullet (•) have sets of private foundation returns (IRS Form 990-PF) for their states or regions, available for public reference.

Because the collections vary in their hours, materials and services, IT IS RECOMMENDED THAT YOU CALL EACH COLLECTION IN ADVANCE.

To check on new locations or current information, call toll-free 1-800-424-9836.

Reference Collections
• The Foundation Center
79 Fifth Ave., 8th Fl.
New York, NY 10003
(212) 620-4230
• The Foundation Center
312 Sutter St., Room 312
San Francisco, CA 94108
(415) 397-0902
• The Foundation Center
1001 Connecticut Ave., NW
Washington, DC 20036
(202) 331-1400
• The Foundation Center
Kent H. Smith Library
1422 Euclid, Suite 1356
Cleveland, OH 44115
(216) 861-1933
• The Foundation Center
Suite 150, Grand Lobby
Hurt Building, 50 Hurt Plaza
Atlanta, GA 30303
(404) 880-0094

**COOPERATING
COLLECTIONS**
Alabama
• Birmingham Public Library
Government Documents
2100 Park Place
Birmingham, AL 35203
(205) 226-3600

Huntsville Public Library
915 Monroe Street
Huntsville, AL 35801
(205) 532-5940
• University of South Alabama
Library Building
Mobile, AL 36688
(205) 460-7025
• Auburn University at
Montgomery Library
7300 University Drive
Montgomery, AL 36117
(334) 244-3653
Alaska
• University of Alaska at
Anchorage, Library
3211 Providence Drive
Anchorage, AK 99508
(907) 786-1848
Juneau Public Library
Reference
292 Marine Way
Juneau, AK 99801
(907) 586-5267
Arizona
• Phoenix Public Library
Business and Sciences Unit
12 E. McDowell Road
Phoenix, AZ 85004
(602) 262-4636

• Tucson Pima Library
101 N. Stone Avenue
Tucson, AZ 85701
(520) 791-4010
Arkansas
• Westark Community College
Borham Library
5210 Grand Avenue
Fort Smith, AR 72913
(501) 788-7200
• Central Arkansas Library Sys.
700 Louisiana Street
Little Rock, AR 72201
(501) 370-5952
Pine Bluff-Jefferson County
Library System
200 East Eighth
Pine Bluff, AR 71601
(501) 534-2159
California
• Humboldt Area Foundation
P.O. Box 99
Bayside, CA 95524
(707) 442-2993
• Ventura Co. Comm. Foundation
Funding and Information
Resource Center
1355 Del Norte Road
Camarillo, CA 93010
(805) 988-0196

• California Community Foundation
Funding Information Center
606 S. Olive Street, Suite 2400
Los Angeles, CA 90014
(213) 413-4042

Oakland Community Fund
Nonprofit Resource Center
1203 Preservation Parkway, Suite 100
Oakland, CA 94612
(510) 834-1010

• Grant and Resource Center of
Northern California
Building C, Suite A
2280 Benton Drive
Redding, CA 96003
(916) 244-1219

Los Angeles Public Library
West Valley Regional Branch Library
19036 Van Owen Street
Reseda, CA 91335
(818) 345-4393

Riverside City and County
Public Library
3021 Franklin Avenue
Riverside, CA 92502
(714) 782-5201

Nonprofit Resource Center
Sacramento Public Library
828 I Street, 2nd Floor
Sacramento, CA 95814
(916) 264-2772

• San Diego Community Foundation
Funding Information Center
101 W. Broadway, Suite 1120
San Diego, CA 92101
(619) 239-8815

• The Foundation Center
312 Sutter Street, Room 312
San Francisco, CA 94108
(415) 397-0902

• Nonprofit Development
Center Library
1922 The Alameda, Suite 212
San Jose, CA 95126
(408) 248-9505

• Peninsula Community Foundation
Funding Information Library
1700 S. El Camino Real, R301
San Mateo, CA 94402
(415) 358-9392

Los Angeles Public Library
San Pedro Regional Branch
9131 S. Gaffey Street
San Pedro, CA 90731
(310) 548-7779

Volunteer Center of Greater
Orange County
Nonprofit Management Assistance Ctr.
1000 E. Santa Ana Blvd., Suite 200
Santa Ana, CA 92701
(714) 953-1655

Santa Barbara Public Library
40 East Anapamu Street
Santa Barbara, CA 93101
(805) 962-7653

Santa Monica Public Library
1343 Sixth Street
Santa Monica, CA 90401
(310) 458-8600

Sonoma County Library
3rd & E Streets
Santa Rosa, CA 95404
(707) 545-0831

Seaside Branch Library
550 Harcourt Street
Seaside, CA 93955
(408) 899-8131

Colorado

Pikes Peak Library District
20 North Cascade Avenue
Colorado Springs, CO 80901
(719) 531-6333

• Denver Public Library
General Reference
10 West 14th Ave. Pkwy.
Denver, CO 80204
(303) 640-6200

Connecticut

Danbury Public Library
170 Main Street
Danbury, CT 06810
(203) 797-4527

• Greenwich Public Library
101 W. Putnam Avenue
Greenwich, CT 06830
(203) 622-7910

• Hartford Public Library
500 Main Street
Hartford, CT 06103
(203) 293-6000

D.A.T.A.
70 Audubon Street
New Haven, CT 06510
(203) 772-1345

Delaware

• University of Delaware
Hugh Morris Library
Newark, DE 19717
(302) 831-2432

District of Columbia

• The Foundation Center
1001 Connecticut Avenue, NW
Washington, DC 20036
(202) 331-1400

Florida

Volusia County Library Center
City Island
Daytona Beach, FL 32014
(904) 255-3765

• Nova Southeastern University
Einstein Library
3301 College Avenue
Ft. Lauderdale, FL 33314
(954) 475-7050

Indian River Comm. College
Charles S. Miley Learning
Resource Center
3209 Virginia Avenue
Ft. Pierce, FL 34981
(407) 462-4757

• Jacksonville Public Library
Grants Resource Center
122 North Ocean Street
Jacksonville, FL 32202
(904) 630-2665

• Miami-Dade Public Library
Humanities/Social Science
101 W. Flagler Street
Miami, FL 33130
(305) 375-5575

• Orlando Public Library
Social Sciences Department
101 E. Central Blvd.
Orlando, FL 32801
(407) 425-4694

Selby Public Library
Reference
1001 Boulevard of the Arts
Sarasota, FL 34236
(813) 951-5501

• Tampa-Hillsborough County
Public Library
900 N. Ashley Drive
Tampa, FL 33602
(813) 273-3628

• Community Foundation for
Palm Beach and Martin Counties
324 Datura Street, Suite 340
West Palm Beach, FL 33401
(407) 659-6800

Georgia

• Atlanta-Fulton Public Library
Foundation Collection
Ivan Allen Department
1 Margaret Mitchell Square
Atlanta, GA 30303
(404) 730-1900

• The Foundation Center
Suite 150, Grand Lobby
Hurt Building, 50 Hurt Plaza
Atlanta, GA 30303
(404) 880-0094
• Dalton Regional Library
310 Cappes Street
Dalton, GA 30720
(706) 278-4507
• Thomas County Public Library
201 N. Madison St.
Thomasville, GA 31792
(912) 225-5252

Hawaii
• University of Hawaii
Hamilton Library
2550 The Mall
Honolulu, HI 96822
(808) 956-7214
Hawaii Community Foundation
Hawaii Resource Center
222 Merchant Street, 2nd Floor
Honolulu, HI 96813
(808) 537-6333

Idaho
• Boise Public Library
715 S. Capitol Blvd.
Boise, ID 83702
(208) 384-4024
• Caldwell Public Library
1010 Dearborn Street
Caldwell, ID 83605
(208) 459-3242

Illinois
• Donors Forum of Chicago
53 W. Jackson Blvd., Suite 430
Chicago, IL 60604
(312) 431-0265
• Evanston Public Library
1703 Orrington Avenue
Evanston, IL 60201
(708) 866-0305
Rock Island Public Library
401 19th Street
Rock Island, IL 61201
(309) 788-7627
• Sangamon State University
Library
Shepherd Road
Springfield, IL 62794
(217) 786-6633

Indiana
• Allen County Public Library
900 Webster Street
Fort Wayne, IN 46802
(219) 424-0544

Indiana University
Northwest Library
3400 Broadway
Gary, IN 46408
(219) 980-6582
• Indianapolis-Marion County
Public Library
Social Sciences
40 E. St. Clair Street
Indianapolis, IN 46206
(317) 269-1733

Iowa
• Cedar Rapids Public Library
Foundation Center Collection
500 First Street, SE
Cedar Rapids, IA 52401
(319) 398-5123
• Southwestern Community
College
Learning Resource Center
1501 W. Townline Road
Creston, IA 50801
(515) 782-7081
• Public Library of Des Moines
100 Locust Street
Des Moines, IA 50309
(515) 283-4152
• Sioux City Public Library
529 Pierce Street
Sioux City, IA 51101
(712) 252-5669

Kansas
• Dodge City Public Library
1001 2nd Avenue
Dodge City, KS 67801
(316) 225-0248
• Topeka and Shawnee County
Public Library
1515 SW Tenth Avenue
Topeka, KS 66604
(913) 233-2040
• Wichita Public Library
223 South Main Street
Wichita, KS 67202
(316) 262-0611

Kentucky
Western Kentucky University
Helm-Cravens Library
Bowling Green, KY 42101
(502) 745-6125
• Lexington Public Library
140 E. Main Street
Lexington, KY 40507
(606) 231-5520

• Louisville Free Public Library
301 York Street
Louisville, KY 40203
(502) 574-1611

Louisiana
• East Baton Rouge Parish Library
Centroplex Branch Grants Collection
120 St. Louis Street
Baton Rouge, LA 70802
(504) 389-4960
• Beauregard Parish Library
205 S. Washington Avenue
De Ridder, LA 70634
(318) 463-6217
• New Orleans Public Library
Business and Science Division
219 Loyola Avenue
New Orleans, LA 70140
(504) 596-2580
• Shreve Memorial Library
424 Texas Street
Shreveport, LA 71120
(318) 226-5894

Maine
• University of Southern Maine
Office of Sponsored Programs
246 Deering Avenue, Room 628
Portland, ME 04103
(207) 780-4871

Maryland
• Enoch Pratt Free Library
Social Science and History Dept.
400 Cathedral Street
Baltimore, MD 21201
(410) 396-5430

Massachusetts
• Associated Grantmakers
of Massachusetts
Suite 840
294 Washington Street
Boston, MA 02108
(617) 426-2606
• Boston Public Library
Social Science Reference
666 Boylston Street
Boston, MA 02117
(617) 536-5400
Western Mass. Funding
Resource Center
65 Elliot Street
Springfield, MA 01101
(413) 732-3175
• Worcester Public Library
Grants Resource Center
Salem Square
Worcester, MA 01608
(508) 799-1655

Michigan

• Alpena County Library
211 N. First Street
Alpena, MI 49707
(517) 356-6188

• University of Michigan
Graduate Library
Reference & Research Services Dept.
Ann Arbor, MI 48109
(313) 764-9373

• Willard Public Library
7 W. Van Buren Street
Battle Creek, MI 49017
(616) 968-8166

• Henry Ford Centennial Library
Adult Services
16301 Michigan Avenue
Dearborn, MI 48126
(313) 943-2330

• Wayne State University
Purdy-Kresge Library
5265 Cass Avenue
Detroit, MI 48202
(313) 577-6424

• Michigan State University Libraries
Social Sciences/Humanities
Main Library
East Lansing, MI 48824
(517) 353-8818

• Farmington Comm. Library
32737 W. 12 Mile Road
Farmington Hills, MI 48018
(810) 553-0300

• University of Michigan
Flint Library
Flint, MI 48502
(810) 762-3408

• Grand Rapids Public Library
Business Department, 3rd Floor
60 Library Plaza NE
Grand Rapids, MI 49503
(616) 456-3600

Michigan Technological University
Van Pelt Library
1400 Townsend Drive
Houghton, MI 49931
(906) 487-2507

Sault Ste. Marie Area
Public Schools
Office of Compensatory Education
460 W. Spruce Street
Sault Ste. Marie, MI 49783
(906) 635-6619

• Northwestern Michigan College
Mark & Helen Osterin Library
1701 E. Front Street
Traverse City, MI 49684
(616) 922-1060

Minnesota

• Duluth Public Library
520 W. Superior Street
Duluth, MN 55802
(218) 723-3802

• Southwest State University
University Library
Marshall, MN 56258
(507) 537-6176

• Minneapolis Public Library
Sociology Department
300 Nicollet Mall
Minneapolis, MN 55401
(612) 372-6555

Rochester Public Library
11 First Street, SE
Rochester, MN 55904
(507) 285-8002

Saint Paul Public Library
90 W. Fourth Street
Saint Paul, MN 55102
(612) 292-6307

Mississippi

• Jackson/Hinds Library System
300 N. State Street
Jackson, MS 39201
(601) 968-5803

Missouri

• Clearinghouse for Midcontinent
Foundations
University of Missouri
5110 Cherry, Suite 310
Kansas City, MO 64110
(816) 235-1176

• Kansas City Public Library
311 E. 12th Street
Kansas City, MO 64106
(816) 221-9650

• Metropolitan Association for
Philanthropy, Inc.
5615 Pershing Avenue, Suite 20
St. Louis, MO 63112
(314) 361-3900

• Springfield-Greene Co. Library
397 E. Central Street
Springfield, MO 65802
(417) 837-5000

Montana

• Montana State University
Library-Special Collections
1500 N. 30th Street
Billings, MT 59101
(406) 657-1662

• Bozeman Public Library
220 E. Lamme
Bozeman, MT 59715
(406) 582-2402

• Montana State Library
Library Services
1515 E. 6th Avenue
Helena, MT 59620
(406) 444-3004

• University of Montana
Maureen & Mike Mansfield Library
Missoula, MT 59812
(406) 243-6800

Nebraska

• University of Nebraska
Love Library
14th and R Streets
Lincoln, NE 68588
(402) 472-2848

• W. Dale Clark Library
Social Sciences Department
215 S. 15th Street
Omaha, NE 68102
(402) 444-4826

Nevada

• Las Vegas-Clark County
Library District
1401 E. Flamingo
Las Vegas, NV 89119
(702) 733-3642

• Washoe County Library
301 S. Center Street
Reno, NV 89501
(702) 785-4010

New Hampshire

• New Hampshire Charitable Fdn.
37 Pleasant Street
Concord, NH 03301
(603) 225-6641

• Plymouth State College
Herbert H. Lamson Library
Plymouth, NH 03264
(603) 535-2258

New Jersey

Cumberland County Library
New Jersey Room
800 E. Commerce Street
Bridgeton, NJ 08302
(609) 453-2210

• Free Public Library of Elizabeth
11 S. Broad Street
Elizabeth, NJ 07202
(908) 354-6060
• County College of Morris
Learning Resource Center
214 Center Grove Road
Randolph, NJ 07869
(201) 328-5296
• New Jersey State Library
Governmental Reference Services
185 W. State Street
Trenton, NJ 08625
(609) 292-6220

New Mexico
• Albuquerque Community
Foundation
3301 Menual, NE, Suite 30
Albuquerque, NM 87176
(505) 883-6240
• New Mexico State Library
Information Services
325 Don Gaspar
Santa Fe, NM 87501
(505) 827-3824

New York
• New York State Library
Humanities Reference
Cultural Education Center
Empire State Plaza
Albany, NY 12230
(518) 474-5355
Suffolk Co-op. Library System
627 N. Sunrise Service Road
Bellport, NY 11713
(516) 286-1600
New York Public Library
Bronx Reference Center
Fordham Branch
2556 Bainbridge Avenue
Bronx, NY 10458
(718) 220-6575
Brooklyn In Touch Information Ctr.
One Hanson Place, Room 2504
Brooklyn, NY 11243
(718) 230-3200
Brooklyn Public Library
Social Sciences Division
Grand Army Plaza
Brooklyn, NY 11238
(718) 780-7700
• Buffalo and Erie County
Public Library
Business and Labor Department
Lafayette Square
Buffalo, NY 14203
(716) 858-7097

Huntington Public Library
338 Main Street
Huntington, NY 11743
(516) 427-5165
Queens Borough Public Library
Social Sciences Division
89-11 Merrick Blvd.
Jamaica, NY 11432
(718) 990-0761
• Levittown Public Library
One Bluegrass Lane
Levittown, NY 11756
(516) 731-5728
New York Public Library
Countee Cullen Branch Library
104 West 136th Street
New York, NY 10030
(212) 491-2070
• Plattsburgh Public Library
19 Oak Street
Plattsburgh, NY 12901
(518) 563-0921
• The Foundation Center
79 Fifth Avenue
New York, NY 10003
(212) 620-4230
Adriance Memorial Library
Special Services Department
93 Market Street
Poughkeepsie, NY 12601
(914) 485-3445
• Rochester Public Library
Business, Economics and Law
115 South Avenue
Rochester, NY 14604
(716) 428-7328
Onondaga Co. Public Library
447 S. Salina Street
Syracuse, NY 13202
(315) 435-1800
Utica Public Library
303 Genesee Street
Utica, NY 13501
(315) 735-2279
White Plains Public Library
100 Martine Avenue
White Plains, NY 10601
(914) 422-1480

North Carolina
• Community Foundation of
Western North Carolina
Learning Resources Center
14 College Street
P.O. Box 1888
Asheville, NC 28801
(704) 254-4960

• The Duke Endowment
100 N. Tryon Street, Suite 3500
Charlotte, NC 28202
(704) 376-0291
Durham County Public Library
301 N. Roxboro Street
Durham, NC 27702
(919) 560-0110
• State Library of North Carolina
Government and Business Services
Archives Building
109 E. Jones Street
Raleigh, NC 27601
(919) 733-3270
• Forsyth Co. Public Library
660 W. 6th Street
Winston-Salem, NC 27101
(910) 727-2680

North Dakota
• Bismarck Public Library
515 N. Fifth Street
Bismarck, ND 58501
(701) 222-6410
• Fargo Public Library
102 N. 3rd Street
Fargo, ND 58102
(701) 241-1491

Ohio
Stark County District Library
Humanities
715 Market Avenue North
Canton, OH 44702
(216) 452-0665
• Public Library of Cincinnati
and Hamilton County
Grants Resource Center
800 Vine Street-Library Square
Cincinnati, OH 45202
(513) 369-6940
• The Foundation Center
Kent H. Smith Library
1422 Euclid Building, Suite 1356
Cleveland, OH 44115
(216) 861-1933
Columbus Metro. Library
Business and Technology
96 S. Grant Ave.
Columbus, OH 43215
(614) 645-2590
• Dayton and Montgomery County
Public Library
Grants Resource Center
215 E. Third Street
Dayton, OH 45402
(513) 227-9500 ext. 211

• Mansfield/Richland County
Public Library
42 W. 3rd Street
Mansfield, OH 44902
(419) 521-3110
• Toledo-Lucas County
Public Library
Social Sciences Department
325 Michigan Street
Toledo, OH 43624
(419) 259-5245
• Youngstown & Mahoning
County Library
305 Wick Avenue
Youngstown, OH 44503
(216) 744-8636
Muskingum County Library
220 N. 5th Street
Zanesville, OH 43701
(614) 453-0391

Oklahoma
• Oklahoma City University
Dulaney Browne Library
2501 N. Blackwelder
Oklahoma City, OK 73106
(405) 521-5072
• Tulsa City-Co. Library System
400 Civic Center
Tulsa, OK 74103
(918) 596-7944

Oregon
Oregon Inst. of Technology Library
3201 Campus Drive
Klamath Falls, OR 97601
(503) 885-1773
• Pacific Non-Profit Network
Grantsmanship Resource Library
33 N. Central, Suite 211
Medford, OR 97501
(503) 779-6044
Multnomah County Library
Government Documents
801 SW Tenth Avenue
Portland, OR 97205
(503) 248-5123
• Oregon State Library
State Library Building
Salem, OR 97310
(503) 378-4277

Pennsylvania
Northampton Community College
Learning Resources Center
3835 Green Pond Road
Bethlehem, PA 18017
(610) 861-5360

Erie County Library System
27 S. Park Row
Erie, PA 16501
(814) 451-6927
Dauphin County Library System
Central Library
101 Walnut Street
Harrisburg, PA 17101
(717) 234-4976
Lancaster County Public Library
125 N. Duke Street
Lancaster, PA 17602
(717) 394-2651
• Free Library of Philadelphia
Regional Foundation Center
Logan Square
Philadelphia, PA 19103
(215) 686-5423
• Carnegie Library of Pittsburgh
Foundation Collection
4400 Forbes Avenue
Pittsburgh, PA 15213
(412) 622-1917
Pocono Northeast Development Fund
James Pettinger Memorial Library
1151 Oak Street
Pittston, PA 18640
(717) 655-5581
Reading Public Library
100 S. Fifth Street
Reading, PA 19602
(610) 655-6355
• Martin Library
159 Market Street
York, PA 17401
(717) 846-5300

Rhode Island
• Providence Public Library
225 Washington Street
Providence, RI 02906
(401) 455-8088

South Carolina
• Anderson County Library
202 E. Greenville Street
Anderson, SC 29621
(803) 260-4500
• Charleston County Library
404 King Street
Charleston, SC 29403
(803) 723-1645
• South Carolina State Library
1500 Senate Street
Columbia, SC 29211
(803) 734-8666

South Dakota
Nonprofit Grants Assistance Center
Business and Education Institute
Washington Street, East Hall
Dakota State University
Madison, SD 57042
(605) 256-5555
• South Dakota State Library
800 Governors Drive
Pierre, SD 57501
(605) 773-5070
(800) 592-1841 (SD residents)
• Sioux Falls Area Foundation
141 N. Main Ave., Suite 310
Sioux Falls, SD 57102
(605) 336-7055

Tennessee
• Knox County Public Library
500 W. Church Avenue
Knoxville, TN 37902
(615) 544-5700
• Memphis & Shelby County
Public Library
1850 Peabody Avenue
Memphis, TN 38104
(901) 725-8877
• Nashville Public Library
Business Information Division
225 Polk Avenue
Nashville, TN 37203
(615) 862-5843

Texas
Abilene center for Nonprofit
Management
Funding Information Library
500 N. Chestnut, Suite 1511
Abilene, TX 79604
(915) 677-8166
• Amarillo Area Foundation
700 First National Place
801 S. Fillmore
Amarillo, TX 79101
(806) 376-4521
• Hogg Foundation for
Mental Health
3001 Lake Austin Blvd.
Austin, TX 78703
(512) 471-5041
Texas A & M University
Library-Reference Dept.
6300 Ocean Drive
Corpus Christi, TX 78412
(512) 994-2608

• Dallas Public Library
Urban Information
1515 Young Street
Dallas, TX 75201
(214) 670-1487
El Paso Community Foundation
201 E. Main Street, Suite 1616
El Paso, TX 79901
(915) 533-4020
• Funding Information Center
Texas Christian University Library
2800 S. University Drive
Ft. Worth, TX 76129
(817) 921-7664
• Houston Public Library
Bibliographic Information Center
500 McKinney Avenue
Houston, TX 77002
(713) 236-1313
• Longview Public Library
222 W. Cotton Street
Longview, TX 75601
(903) 237-1352
Lubbock Area Foundation, Inc.
1655 Main Street, Suite 209
Lubbock, TX 79401
(806) 762-8061
• Funding Information Center
530 McCullough, Suite 600
San Antonio, TX 78212
(210) 227-4333
• North Texas Center for
Nonprofit Management
624 Indiana, Suite 307
Wichita Falls, TX 76301
(817) 322-4961
Utah
• Salt Lake City Public Library
209 E. 500 South
Salt Lake City, UT 84111
(801) 524-8200
Vermont
• Vermont Department of Libraries
Reference & Law Info. Services
109 State Street
Montpelier, VT 05609
(802) 828-3268
Virginia
Hampton Public Library
4207 Victoria Blvd.
Hampton, VA 23669
(804) 727-1312

• Richmond Public Library
Business, Science & Technology
Department
101 E. Franklin Street
Richmond, VA 23219
(804) 780-8223
• Roanoke City Public
Library System
Central Library
706 S. Jefferson Street
Roanoke, VA 24016
(703) 981-2477
Washington
• Mid-Columbia Library
405 S. Dayton
Kennewick, WA 99336
(509) 586-3156
• Seattle Public Library
Science, Social Science
1000 Fourth Avenue
Seattle, WA 98104
(206) 386-4620
• Spokane Public Library
Funding Information Center
West 811 Main Avenue
Spokane, WA 99201
(509) 626-5347
• United Way of Pierce County
Center for Nonprofit Development
734 Broadway
P.O. Box 2215
Tacoma, WA 98401
(206) 597-6686
Greater Wenatchee Community
Foundation at the Wenatchee
Public Library
310 Douglas Street
Wenatchee, WA 98807
(509) 662-5021
West Virginia
• Kanawha County Public Library
123 Capitol Street
Charleston, WV 25301
(304) 343-4646
Wisconsin
• University of Wisconsin
Memorial Library
728 State Street
Madison, WI 53706
(608) 262-3242
• Marquette University
Memorial Library
Funding Information Center
1415 W. Wisconsin Avenue
Milwaukee, WI 53201
(414) 288-1515

• University of Wisconsin
Library-Foundation Collection
99 Reserve Street
Stevens Point, WI 54481
(715) 346-3826
Wyoming
• Natrona County Public Library
307 East 2nd Street
Casper, WY 82601
(307) 237-4935
• Laramie Co. Community College
Instructional Resource Center
1400 E. College Drive
Cheyenne, WY 82007
(307) 778-1206
• Campbell County Public Library
2101 4-J Road
Gillette, WY 82716
(307) 682-3223
• Teton County Library
320 South King Street
Jackson, WY 83001
(307) 733-2164
Rock Springs Library
400 C Street
Rock Springs, WY 82901
(307) 352-6667

Puerto Rico
University of Puerto Rico
Ponce Technological College
Library
Box 7186
Ponce, PR 00732
(809) 844-8181
Universidad Del Sagrado
Corazon
M.M.T. Guevara Library
Santurce, PR 00914
(809) 728-1515 ext. 4357

Appendix B

The Grantsmanship Center

The Grantsmanship Center is the world's oldest and largest training organization for the nonprofit sector. Since it was founded in 1972, the Center has trained more than 60,000 staff members of public and private agencies in grantsmanship, program management and fund-raising.

The five-day Grantsmanship Training Program, first offered in 1972 and continuously updated, began a new era in training seminars and workshops for nonprofit agencies. Over 30,000 nonprofit agency staff members have attended this demanding, week-long workshop, the single most widely attended training program in the history of the nonprofit sector. It covers all aspects of researching for grants, writing grant proposals, and negotiating with funding sources.

The Grant Proposal Writing Workshop, an intensive three-day laboratory, teaches you how to write a good proposal and plan better programs at the same time, using the Grantsmanship Center's program planning and proposal writing format.

The Center also produces publications on grantsmanship, planning, fund-raising, management, and personnel issues for nonprofit agencies. Its Program Planning and Proposal Writing booklet is now a classic in the field and has been used by hundreds of thousands of successful grant seekers.

For detailed information about The Grantsmanship Center's training programs, publications, and other services to the nonprofit sector, write to The Grantsmanship Center, Dept. DD, P.O. Box 17220, Los Angeles, CA 90017 and ask for a free copy of *The Grantsmanship Center Magazine*.

Index to Foundations

(Alphabetical)

Citations are by entry number

A

Abbott Laboratories Fund, 141

Abell Foundation, Inc., 188

Ahmanson Foundation, 12

Air Products Foundation, 388

Akron Community Foundation, 338

Akron Jaycee Foundation, 339

Alcoa Foundation, 389

Allegheny Foundation, 390

AlliedSignal Foundation, 261

Altman Foundation, 275

Ameritech Foundation, 142

Anderson (Peyton) Foundation, Inc., 121

Annenberg Foundation, 391

ARCO Foundation, 13

Area Fund, 276

Arvin Foundation, Inc., 161

Ashbrook (Mary K.) Foundation for El Reno, Oklahoma, 372

Ashtabula Foundation, Inc., 340

AT&T Foundation, 277

Atherton Family Foundation, 130

Atkinson Foundation, 14

B

Badgeley (Rose M.) Residuary Charitable Trust, 278

Ball Brothers Foundation, 162

Baltimore Community Foundation, 189

Bank IV Charitable Trust, 181

BankAmerica Foundation, 15

Barker (Donald R.) Foundation, Inc., 16

Barra Foundation, Inc., 392

Baton Rouge Area Foundation, 185

Battle Creek Community Foundation, 201

Bauervic-Paisley Foundation, 202

Baughman Foundation, 182

Baumker (Elsie and Harry) Charitable Fdn., 341

Bayer Foundation, 393

Beattie (Cordelia Lee) Foundation Trust, 104

Beazley Foundation, Inc., 474

Beckley Area Foundation, Inc., 490

Beckman (Arnold and Mabel) Foundation, 17

Beckman (Leland D.) Foundation, 138

Bedsole (J.L.) Foundation, 1

BellSouth Foundation, 122

Beloit Foundation, Inc., 143

Berger (H.N. and Frances C.) Foundation, 18

Besser Foundation, 203

Bigelow (F.R.) Foundation, 222

Bingham (William) Foundation, 342

Bishop (A.G.) Charitable Trust, 204

Blandin Foundation, 223

Blount Foundation, Inc., 2

Blowitz-Ridgeway Foundation, 144

Bodman Foundation, 279

Boettcher Foundation, 71

Booth Ferris Foundation, 280

Boston Foundation, Inc., 193

Bothin Foundation, 19

Bradley (Lynde and Harry) Foundation, Inc., 493

Bremer (Otto) Foundation, 224

Bromley (Guy I.) Residuary Trust, 238

Broward Community Foundation, Inc., 105

Brown Foundation, Inc., 434

Bruening (Eva L. and Joseph M.) Foundation, 343

Bryan (Kathleen Price and Joseph M.) Family Foundation, 322

Buchanan Family Foundation, 145

Buehler (Emil) Perpetual Trust, 262

Buffalo Foundation, 281

Buhl Foundation, 394

Burkitt Foundation, 435

Burroughs Wellcome Fund, 323

Bush (Edyth) Charitable Foundation, Inc., 106

Bush Foundation, 225

C

Cabot Corporation Foundation, Inc., 194

Cafritz (Morris and Gwendolyn) Foundation, 96

Calder (Louis) Foundation, 282

California Community Foundation, 20

Campbell (J. Bulow) Foundation, 123

Canaan Fdn. for Christian Education, 471

Index to Foundations

(Subject Index)

Citations are by entry number

COMPUTER GRANTS—3, 4, 5, 6, 9, 10, 11, 12, 13, 15, 16, 18, 19, 21, 22, 23, 25, 27, 28, 29, 33, 34, 35, 38, 39, 41, 44, 45, 46, 47, 50, 51, 52, 54, 56, 57, 58, 59, 60, 61, 62, 63, 64, 65, 67, 68, 69, 70, 72, 73, 74, 75, 77, 78, 79, 80, 81, 84, 88, 89, 90, 91, 92, 93, 94, 95, 98, 99, 104, 105, 106, 107, 108, 109, 110, 111, 112, 115, 117, 118, 120, 123, 124, 127, 128, 130, 132, 133, 134, 135, 136, 137, 138, 139, 140, 143, 146, 148, 149, 152, 154, 157, 159, 160, 162, 164, 165, 166, 168, 170, 171, 173, 174, 175, 176, 178, 180, 182, 183, 184, 185, 187, 188, 189, 190, 191, 192, 195, 198, 199, 200, 201, 203, 204, 205, 208, 210, 211, 212, 214, 216, 217, 218, 220, 222, 224, 231, 235, 237, 238, 240, 245, 247, 248, 249, 250, 252, 253, 255, 256, 257, 258, 259, 260, 265, 266, 267, 268, 270, 274, 278, 281, 285, 286, 287, 288, 289, 290, 291, 293, 295, 296, 298, 300, 302, 309, 311, 316, 319, 320, 321, 325, 326, 327, 330, 331, 333, 334, 336, 338, 339, 342, 345, 347, 348, 350, 352, 353, 354, 355, 358, 359, 360, 362, 363, 364, 365, 366, 367, 369, 372, 373, 375, 378, 379, 381, 384, 387, 393, 394, 395, 396, 398, 399, 402, 403, 404, 407, 408, 411, 415, 416, 417, 421, 422, 423, 425, 426, 427, 429, 430, 431, 432, 435, 436, 437, 440, 444, 450, 452, 453, 458, 459, 460, 462, 464, 465, 467, 469, 470, 471, 473, 474, 475, 477, 480, 482, 483, 484, 487, 488, 489, 490, 491, 492, 494, 497, 499, 503, 504

CULTURAL PROGRAMS—3, 4, 7, 10, 12, 18, 19, 22, 24, 29, 38, 39, 43, 46, 47, 49, 52, 56, 64, 67, 74, 75, 79, 80, 83, 84, 93, 95, 101, 104, 105, 115, 125, 130, 131, 132, 133, 134, 139, 141, 142, 145, 147, 151, 155, 156, 158, 159, 160, 164, 167, 174, 177, 189, 194, 198, 199, 200, 201, 212, 227, 228, 232, 234, 239, 257, 262, 266, 276, 284, 287, 292, 296, 300, 307, 311, 319, 320, 324, 325, 326, 329, 331, 338, 345, 359, 365, 374, 378, 382, 383, 386, 387, 395, 396, 412, 421, 437, 448, 450, 453, 456, 475, 476, 477, 478, 479, 483, 493, 501

DISABLED—3, 4, 9, 18, 19, 21, 25, 27, 33, 34, 37, 50, 56, 57, 59, 63, 70, 73, 74, 75, 80, 81, 92, 96, 97, 103, 105, 111, 115, 127, 134, 137, 144, 159, 160, 183, 187, 190, 193, 206, 227, 229, 239, 244, 256, 265, 282, 308, 310, 325, 345, 348, 352, 366, 380, 394, 402, 412, 415, 429, 436, 440, 449, 450, 458, 459, 460, 475, 483, 484, 487, 490, 491, 494, 502

EDUCATION (other than higher education)—1, 2, 6, 10, 11, 12, 14, 18, 21, 29, 33, 37, 44, 45, 46, 47, 51, 57, 69, 70, 76, 77, 79, 81, 82, 87, 89, 92, 94, 96, 99, 102, 103, 104, 107, 109, 118, 119, 120, 121, 122, 123, 127, 129, 130, 136, 138, 139, 142, 148, 152, 154, 157, 158, 160, 165, 168, 169, 170, 171, 175, 178, 180, 183, 186, 187, 188, 189, 190, 191, 192, 193, 195, 203, 205, 208, 213, 214, 215, 218, 227, 231, 249, 256, 257, 258, 260, 263, 268, 275, 279, 281, 282, 293, 297, 299, 300, 302, 314, 317, 318, 322, 326, 328, 329, 332, 335, 338, 344, 345, 346, 347, 350, 355, 358, 359, 364, 365, 366, 367, 370, 372, 377, 378, 379, 382, 384, 389, 394, 395, 396, 397, 400, 403, 411, 422, 427, 428, 438, 439, 443, 444, 446, 450, 451, 454, 457, 463, 471, 473, 475, 482, 489, 490, 491, 494, 495, 496, 502, 503, 504

ENGINEERING—2, 13, 30, 31, 33, 40, 49, 50, 66, 71, 76, 78, 81, 82, 83, 85, 86, 87, 116, 122, 141, 142, 153, 160, 161, 172, 194, 196, 207, 209, 215, 219, 225, 226, 228, 232, 234, 242, 244, 246, 261, 264, 269, 277, 283, 289, 291, 293, 297, 304, 305, 308, 317, 349, 351, 356, 357, 359, 371, 376, 383, 386, 388, 389, 391, 393, 409, 412, 413, 414, 418, 419, 420, 434, 438, 442, 447, 455, 456, 461, 468, 487, 489, 493, 500

HEALTH ORGANIZATIONS—6, 16, 19, 26, 35, 36, 45, 51, 56, 58, 61, 68, 72, 74, 81, 90, 91, 106, 108, 110, 118, 127, 130, 137, 142, 156, 163, 166, 185, 191, 205, 206, 233, 247, 252, 258,

266, 267, 268, 270, 284, 294, 296, 298, 309, 315, 321, 326, 327, 333, 334, 336, 339, 341, 352, 354, 360, 361, 367, 369, 378, 384, 387, 398, 405, 411, 429, 432, 439, 450, 452, 453, 459, 460, 484, 488, 498, 499

HIGHER EDUCATION—2, 6, 8, 10, 12, 13, 15, 18, 24, 30, 31, 33, 36, 39, 40, 41, 42, 43, 49, 50, 61, 64, 65, 66, 67, 70, 71, 73, 78, 82, 83, 84, 85, 86, 91, 92, 94, 100, 106, 112, 113, 114, 119, 122, 124, 141, 148, 151, 160, 161, 162, 168, 171, 172, 174, 180, 181, 194, 196, 198, 201, 206, 207, 209, 215, 216, 218, 222, 223, 224, 225, 226, 232, 234, 242, 243, 245, 246, 250, 251, 257, 261, 264, 269, 270, 271, 275, 277, 279, 280, 283, 286, 289, 291, 292, 294, 296, 297, 302, 304, 305, 306, 308, 312, 322, 323, 324, 327, 342, 345, 349, 350, 351, 353, 357, 363, 371, 372, 374, 375, 376, 379, 381, 383, 386, 388, 389, 390, 392, 393, 401, 402, 406, 409, 410, 412, 414, 417, 418, 419, 420, 426, 434, 435, 442, 443, 445, 446, 447, 450, 451, 454, 455, 456, 457, 458, 461, 463, 466, 467, 468, 470, 472, 477, 478, 482, 487, 489, 492, 493, 500

HIGH-TECH OFFICE EQUIPMENT—3, 9, 12, 14, 19, 21, 24, 26, 27, 35, 37, 45, 51, 56, 60, 63, 72, 79, 90, 106, 112, 130, 133, 134, 137, 149, 159, 166, 168, 171, 179, 185, 188, 197, 201, 204, 205, 208, 210, 216, 235, 247, 258, 265, 273, 276, 284, 290, 294, 295, 310, 311, 316, 318, 319, 321, 322, 325, 338, 339, 340, 341, 352, 365, 369, 370, 373, 378, 380, 384, 402, 405, 411, 423, 429, 437, 449, 451, 460, 464, 481, 482, 484, 488, 490, 491

LIBRARIES—6, 18, 24, 39, 41, 46, 69, 73, 80, 91, 93, 94, 105, 112, 113, 114, 124, 129, 138, 140, 168, 170, 176, 179, 182, 184, 198, 210, 216, 217, 224, 230, 241, 248, 250, 251, 254, 256, 281, 284, 305, 316, 319, 321, 354, 368, 381, 382, 390, 401, 404, 406, 409, 411, 417, 421, 425, 426, 450, 470, 477, 482, 492, 497

SCIENCE—1, 2, 5, 6, 7, 8, 10, 13, 15, 17, 24, 30, 31, 33, 37, 39, 42, 43, 47, 49, 50, 54, 55, 61, 64, 66, 69, 70, 71, 75, 76, 78, 81, 82, 83, 85, 86, 87, 94, 96, 100, 107, 109, 112, 114, 116, 119, 123, 124, 125, 128, 129, 141, 142, 145, 147, 151, 153, 154, 155, 156, 158, 160, 161, 162, 165, 172, 177, 180, 186, 189, 192, 194, 196, 199, 200, 201, 207, 209, 213, 215, 216, 218, 219, 221, 222, 223, 225, 226, 227, 228, 232, 234, 239, 242, 243, 244, 246, 257, 260, 261, 262, 263, 264, 269, 270, 271, 272, 275, 277, 279, 280, 282, 283, 284, 289, 291, 292, 293, 296, 297, 299, 300, 302, 303, 304, 306, 307, 308, 309, 310, 312, 317, 320, 323, 324, 328, 329, 332, 335, 337, 346, 349, 351, 357, 359, 371, 374, 375, 377, 379, 381, 382, 383, 385, 386, 387, 388, 389, 390, 391, 392, 393, 396, 400, 401, 404, 407, 409, 410, 412, 413, 414, 418, 419, 420, 426, 428, 434, 438, 439, 441, 442, 443, 446, 447, 448, 454, 455, 456, 457, 458, 459, 461, 468, 472, 475, 476, 478, 479, 482, 485, 486, 487, 489, 491, 492, 493, 501

SOCIAL SERVICE ORGANIZATIONS—4, 9, 20, 26, 27, 35, 37, 40, 45, 46, 48, 50, 51, 54, 56, 59, 63, 78, 79, 84, 93, 94, 98, 110, 111, 113, 115, 118, 120, 123, 126, 133, 134, 138, 143, 146, 149, 159, 166, 168, 170, 175, 182, 185, 187, 201, 205, 208, 210, 217, 222, 231, 236, 238, 240, 241, 247, 255, 266, 285, 290, 319, 334, 337, 338, 339, 344, 354, 358, 366, 373, 381, 397, 402, 415, 429, 437, 452, 453, 464, 465, 477, 480, 483, 484, 490, 492, 499

SOFTWARE—12, 18, 20, 32, 40, 47, 50, 51, 56, 60, 65, 67, 73, 74, 75, 79, 81, 93, 94, 102, 104, 106, 115, 118, 126, 127, 130, 133, 138, 139, 146, 148, 159, 167, 168, 170, 173, 182, 183, 189, 191, 197, 208, 210, 217, 230, 233, 235, 236, 240, 260, 266, 281, 293, 310, 311, 319, 320, 321, 325, 327, 340, 348, 350, 352, 353, 365, 384, 397, 399, 402, 407, 411, 417, 422, 424, 433, 435, 437, 452, 475, 489, 491, 494, 496, 498

YOUTH—9, 12, 13, 16, 25, 27, 33, 34, 37, 44, 45, 51, 57, 59, 63, 68, 69, 75, 81, 87, 88, 100, 103, 106, 115, 118, 123, 125, 133, 156, 158, 159, 166, 168, 173, 190, 192, 193, 205, 227, 231, 247, 255, 266, 270, 278, 281, 282, 289, 291, 309, 316, 326, 368, 384, 408, 417, 429, 437, 450, 452, 460, 476, 483, 498, 501, 502